MW01125747

To: _____

From: _____

Date: _____

TRUE HEART GIRLS
DEVOTIONAL

Thinking God's Way!

Sherry Kyle

True Heart Girls Devotional: Thinking God's Way!

RoseKidz® is an imprint of
Rose Publishing, LLC
P.O. Box 3473
Peabody, Massachusetts 01961-3473 USA
www.hendricksonrose.com/rosekidz
All rights reserved.

Book layout design by Drew McCall
Book cover by Emily Heintz

Managing Editor, Karen McGraw
Editorial Assistant, Talia Messina
Contributing Editor, Drew McCall

Published in association with Books & Such Literary Management, 52 Mission Circle #122, PMB 170, Santa Rosa, California 95409, www.booksandsuch.com.

ISBN: 978-1-62862-784-8
RoseKidz® Reorder #L50023
JUVENILE NONFICTION/Religious/Christian/Devotion & Prayer

Printed in the United States of America
Printed August 2019

Contents

Introduction...7

CHAPTER 1: Be Full of Joy..9

CHAPTER 2: Be Considerate..21

CHAPTER 3: Don't Worry about Anything..33

CHAPTER 4: Pray about Everything...45

CHAPTER 5: What Is True..57

CHAPTER 6: What Is Honorable...69

CHAPTER 7: What Is Right...81

CHAPTER 8: What Is Pure..93

CHAPTER 9: What Is Lovely..105

CHAPTER 10: What Is Admirable...117

CHAPTER 11: What Is Excellent...129

CHAPTER 12: What Is Worthy of Praise..141

CHAPTER 13: God's Peace...153

Answer Keys...165

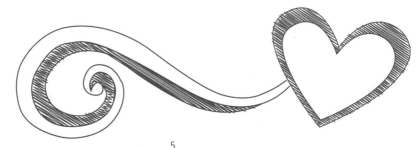

Introduction

Hey, Friend!

Are you joyful?

No, I'm not asking you how you FEEL. Our mood can change from day to day, and sometimes hour by hour. Sometimes the weather can make us feel a little down, and if we're sick or going through something really challenging, we can feel downright miserable.

So, what is being joyful all about?

You can find joy and peace by relying on God and changing the way you THINK. Did you know people have 60,000 thoughts per day? That's a lot of thinking! And guess what? 48,000 of those thoughts are usually negative. But you can change that number by fixing your thoughts on what God says is important from Philippians 4:4–10: what is true, honorable, right, and pure, to name a few things.

True Heart Girls Devotional: *Thinking God's Way* will not only guide you through Scripture, but also give you stories about girls your age, questions to consider, a journaling section to write (or doodle), and some fun activities to explore.

So what are you waiting for?

Discover how to think God's way right now!

Your friend,

Sherry Kyle

Secret Message

To decode the secret message, fill out all the missing words after reading the Bible stories. Find the numbered boxes and write them on the appropriate line below. The last letter has been given to you.

___ ___ - ___ ___ ___ ___ ___ ___
  1   2   3   4   5   6   7   8

___ ___ ___ ___ ___ s!
  9   10   11   12   13

There is an answer key on page 165.

BE FULL OF JOY

> (Dear) sisters, you will face all kinds of trouble. When you do, think of it as pure joy. Your faith will be tested. You know that when this happens it will produce in you the strength to continue.
>
> JAMES 1:2-3

Savannah's Troubles

Savannah woke up, washed her face, and wiggled into her favorite clothes. Her mom and dad started arguing during breakfast, which made Savannah late for school.

When she walked into class, Ethan was showing everyone his science project. No one would've noticed she was tardy if she hadn't tripped over the power cord and bumped into his desk just as Ethan's volcano erupted. Bright orange lava goo sprayed several kids in the front row—as well as Mr. Foster, her teacher!

Everyone gasped, and Ethan sent her a look that made her shiver. Savannah stood up, swiped goo off her right cheek, and tried to pick the volcano up off the floor. "Sorry," she squeaked.

As he tried to wipe some goo off his sweatshirt, Ethan said, "Oh, by the way, the dye is permanent."

Now at lunch, Savannah wanted to reverse time and hide in bed. She ate the last bite of her sandwich and dug in the paper bag for her apple. After a few bites, Jessica walked up and sat beside her.

"We wondered where you were," Jessica said, gesturing to some girls sitting across the room. "We heard about Ethan's volcano."

Savannah cringed and covered the neon spot on her T-shirt with her arm. "Not my best moment."

Jessica lifted a shoulder. "It was an accident. Could've happened to anyone."

"Says the girl who doesn't have bright orange lava goo on her clothes—"

"No one else looks upset. Is something else bothering you?"

Savannah could never hide anything from Jessica, her best friend since forever. She blinked back tears. "My mom and dad had another fight this morning. A big one. I'm afraid they're going to split up."

Jessica put an arm around her shoulder. "I'm sorry. That's rough." Her eyes brightened. "I know what you need. Come sit by us. Emma baked cookies!"

Savannah smiled. "Thanks for cheering me up."

Later that night, Savannah wrote in her journal.

> Dear God,
>
> Today was not a good day, but I'm thankful for my friends, especially Jessica. I'm also grateful that Ethan didn't beat me up for ruining his volcano! I'm still scared about what might happen with my parents, but I'm happy that I can talk to you.
>
> Love,
>
> Savannah

Your Turn

1. Describe a difficult situation you are going through right now.

2. Who is someone in your life you can talk to?

3. Name three things you are thankful for.

Did You Know?

Plants need to be cut back, or *pruned*, to make them grow. Some flowering plants only need the dead parts removed, while other plants benefit from being completely cut down to the ground. But how can this be good for the plant? Doesn't it kill it?

Pruning actually stimulates healthy growth. Flowering plants produce more flowers, and fruit trees produce larger and healthier fruit. The key is to know when to prune. But even if you prune at the wrong time, most plants will recover.

Did you know God prunes us too? He allows the tough stuff in our lives to build our character. Romans 5:3–5 says,

> We are full of joy even when we suffer. We know that our suffering gives us the strength to go on. The strength to go on produces character. Character produces hope. And hope will never bring us shame. That's because God's love has been poured into our hearts. This happened through the Holy Spirit, who has been given to us.

Try This!

Spend some time doing yard work at home. Check with your parents and find out what jobs they'd like you to do and what equipment you can use. You may find out you have a green thumb!

Below is a list of ten yard and garden tools you might use to get the job done. Uncode the words on the next page by writing the letter alphabetically BEFORE the letter under the blank line. The definitions can help you solve the codes.

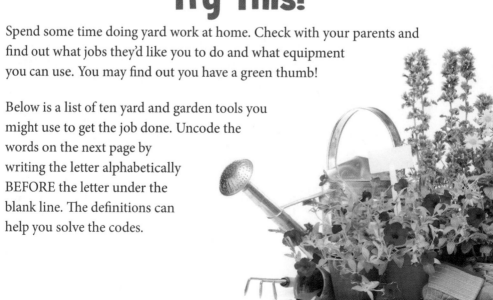

1. W H _ _ _ _ _ _ _ _ _
   x i f f m c b s s p x
   a cart with one wheel and two handles.

2. _ _ _ _ _ _ _ _ _ _ _
   h b s e f o u s p x f m
   a flat-bladed hand tool used to break up soil and dig small holes.

3. _ _ _ _ _ _ _ _ _ _ _
   h b s e f o h m p w f t
   protection for the hands from water and dirt.

4. _ _ _ _ _ _ _ _ _ _ _
   q s v o j o h t i f b s t
   a type of scissors used on plants.

5. _ _ _ _ _ _ _
   m p q q f s t
   a cutting tool, used for pruning trees or small branches.

6. _ _ _ _ _ _ _ _ _
   h b s e f o i p t f
   a flexible tube used to water plants.

7. _ _ _ _ _ _ _ _ _
   h b s e f o g p s l
   tool with four long, strong prongs with sharp points to dig in hard soil.

8. _ _ _ _ _ _ _ _
   m f b g s b l f
   a tool shaped like a fan used to glide over grass and collect leaves.

9. _ _ _ _ _ _ _ _ _ _ _ _ _ _
   t r v b s f q p j o u t i p w f m
   a flat-edged shovel used to lift and move heavier loads.

10. _ _ _ _ _
    t q b e f
    a hand tool used to dig, loosen, or break up lumps in the soil.

Answer key on page 165.

Do It!

Character Dot-to-Dot

Try this dot-to-dot puzzle and consider how God prunes us to build our character! Use a pencil to connect the dots, and then trace over the lines and color in the picture with crayons or colored pencils.

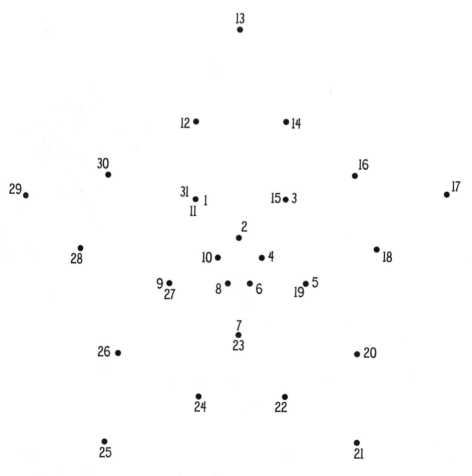

Answer key on page 165.

Because you know all this, you have great joy. You have joy even though you may have had to suffer for a little while.

1 Peter 1:6–8

Bible Story

JOB

Job 1:1–3, 13–22

A long time ago in Bible times, a man named Job lived in the land of Uz. He was a man of integrity who loved God and followed his laws. He had ten children in all, seven sons and three daughters, and was the richest person in the entire area. He owned seven thousand sheep, three thousand camels, five hundred teams of oxen, and five hundred female donkeys. He also had many servants.

One day, when Job's sons and daughters were feasting, a messenger arrived and said, "Your oxen were plowing, with the donkeys feeding beside them, when the Sabeans attacked us. They stole all the animals and killed all the farmhands. I am the only one who escaped to tell you."

Before the second messenger finished speaking, another messenger arrived and said, "The fire of God has fallen from heaven and burned up your sheep and all the shepherds. I am the only one who escaped to tell you."

And before THAT man finished speaking, a third messenger arrived. He said, "Three bands of Chaldean raiders have stolen your camels and killed your servants. I am the only one who escaped to tell you."

And before the third messenger finished speaking, a FOURTH messenger appeared. He said, "Your sons and daughters were feasting in their oldest brother's home. Suddenly a powerful wind swept in from the wilderness and hit the house on all sides. The house collapsed, and all your children are dead. I am the only one who escaped to tell you."

Job stood and tore his robe in grief. He shaved his head and fell to the ground to worship God. He said,

> I came naked from my mother's womb,
> and I will be naked when I leave.
> The Lord gave me what I had,
> and the Lord has taken it away.
> Praise the name of the Lord!

In spite of all of the terrible things that happened to him, Job did not sin and turn away from God.

Your Turn

1. When was the last time something was taken away from you?

2. Did you blame God or were you able to praise
   him even though you were sad or upset?

Do It!

Just as Job was able to praise God during difficult times, you too can have joy when your faith is tested. Create this terrarium and consider how flowers bloom after a season of bare branches.

Glass Jar Terrarium

WHaT YOU NeeD

- Colored tissue paper (three different colors, including green)
- Hot glue gun
- Glass mason jar with lid
- Small twig, shorter than the mason jar

WHaT YOU DO

1. Crumple small pieces of green tissue paper and glue them to the underside of the mason jar lid, creating the grass.

2. Tear off tiny pieces of the other two colors of tissue paper, then crumple them. Glue crumpled tissue paper to the twig's branches, creating flowers.

3. Glue the end of the twig to the middle of the grassy side of the mason-jar lid.

4. Place the glass mason jar over the small tree and screw on the lid.

aLTerNaTe IDea

If you don't have a jar, cut a small piece of cardboard and create the same scene gluing everything to the cardboard instead of a lid.

Bible Story

JOB

Job 1:1-3, 13-22

Find the Missing Word

___ ___ ___ was an honest man.

Write about It

God commands us to be joyful during the hard times. Use the space below to write (or doodle) about a time you worshiped God and thanked him for all he has done for you.

Tiny Treasure

Like pruning, God uses trials to grow our faith and make us strong.

Prayer

Lord God, thank you for giving me joy during the hard times. Help me to praise you always. In Jesus' name, amen.

Be Considerate

> None of you should look out
> just for your own good. Each of you
> should also look out for the good of others.
>
> PHILIPPIANS 2:4

Brianna's Battle

Brianna snatched another cookie out of the cookie jar. She couldn't resist her mom's snickerdoodles. The cinnamon-sugar coating melted in her mouth.

Brianna reached for another when her mom walked into the kitchen. "I hope you're not eating the cookies. They're for the bake sale to pay for the school's new math tutor—who just might be your Aunt Molly."

Brianna gave her a sheepish grin. Oops!

Mom's cell phone rang. As she answered it, Brianna escaped to her room.

Brianna flopped back on her star-patterned quilt almost squishing Roxie. The small dog jumped down. Brianna could offer to feed Roxie, but her mom usually told her when it was time. For the next twenty minutes, Brianna read a book, listened to music, and daydreamed about winning the girls' baseball championship.

Then Brianna glanced around her room. What a mess! Mom had told her numerous times to clean the clutter. Maybe she could pick it up a little. She grabbed a pile of dirty clothes off her floor, dusted her dresser and bookshelf, and tidied up her desk. Brianna smiled. Her mom was right. A clean room made her feel good.

Roxie lay next to the door, her head between her two front paws.

"You hungry, girl? Let's go eat!" Brianna opened the door and ran down the hallway to the kitchen. She scooped up the dog's dish and filled it with dry dog food.

Mom turned off the water and dried her hands on a towel. "Thank you, Brianna. And I didn't have to remind you today."

"I know how busy you are," Brianna said. "Plus, it's my job to feed the dog. Oh, and I cleaned my room, too."

Mom leaned against the counter. "What brought this on?"

"I realized it's not fair that I wait for you to ask me to do my chores when I should be doing them on my own."

"That's very considerate of you." Mom said.

Later that night, Brianna wrote in her journal.

> Dear God,
>
> I found out my aunt Molly might be the new math tutor if our school raises enough money from the bake sale! Thank goodness I didn't eat all the snickerdoodles. I'm going to see how many days in a row I can keep my room clean and feed the dog without being asked. Felt good to have Mom say I was being considerate.
>
> Love,
>
> Brianna

Your Turn

1. Do you sneak cookies, have a messy room, or forget to feed your family pet like Brianna? Write about it here.

2. Name a weekly chore you will do on your own without being asked.

3. Write about a time you put others first. How did it make you feel?

Did You Know?

Putting others first is not a natural response, but a choice we make to help others. Guess what? As his followers, God has given us the Holy Spirit to help us. The Holy Spirit helps us grow certain characteristics that are called the fruit of the Spirit. These characteristics are described in Galatians 5:22–23:

> *But the fruit the Holy Spirit produces is love, joy and peace. It is being patient, kind and good. It is being faithful and gentle and having control of oneself. There is no law against things of that kind.*

Putting others first is one example of growing the fruit of the Spirit. It can be an example of patience, kindness, goodness, gentleness, and self-control—five fruit in one!

Try This!

Look for ways you can show the fruit of the Holy Spirit to those around you. Can you show patience to your sibling? Kindness to a friend? Gentleness to your pet? How about showing your mom or dad how much you love them? If you have a difficult time doing any of these, ask the Holy Spirit to help you.

Below are some specific ideas (some big, some small) of ways to put others first. Rank them from easiest (one) to most difficult (ten). When you've completed one of these ideas, write about it in a journal or on a separate sheet of paper. Be sure to include specifics of what happened as well as how you were feeling before, during, and after.

- ☐ Be happy for someone else's achievements.
- ☐ Be on time!
- ☐ Consider other people's feelings.
- ☐ Copy the actions of a selfless person you know.
- ☐ Find out more about issues that concern you, such as feeding the hungry, helping those who need assistance, or donating material goods to a charity such as an animal shelter.
- ☐ Forgive someone who has hurt you.
- ☐ Let someone else go first.
- ☐ Listen when other people are talking.
- ☐ Show kindness or give something of yours away.
- ☐ Volunteer to do chores at home or help your teacher at school.

In order to put others first, you need to make sure you take care of yourself, too. If you aren't healthy, you won't be strong enough to take care of other people.

Do It!

Quilt Coloring

Design a quilt like Brianna's by coloring in the sections of this quilt pattern. Do you have a blanket that you or your family is not using? Consider giving it to someone in need.

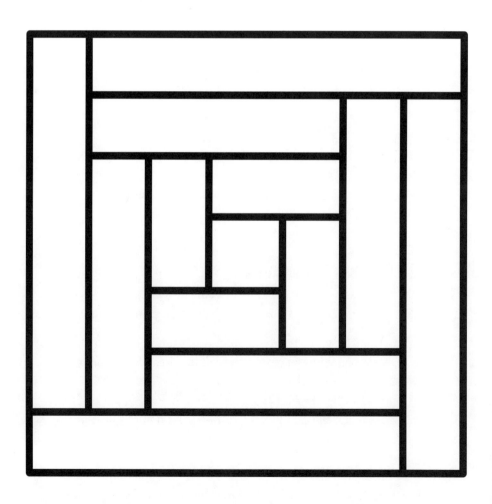

The cheerful look of a messenger brings joy to your heart. And good news gives health to your body.

PrOVerBS 15:30

Bible Story

THE GOOD SamariTan
Luke 10:25-37

A Temple authority asked Jesus how he could receive eternal life.

"What does the Law say?" Jesus asked.

"To love God with all my heart and to love my neighbor as myself. But who is my neighbor?" asked the man.

Jesus smiled. He knew this man wanted praise and recognition for being a worship leader. The man thought his neighbors were people like him. Instead of answering him directly, Jesus told the following parable, or story:

Bandits attacked a Jewish man as he traveled from Jerusalem to Jericho. They tore off his clothes, beat him up, and left him for dead on the side of the road.

When a priest saw the injured man lying there, he went to the other side of the road and passed right by. Next, a Temple assistant walked over and saw the man lying there, and he, too, passed by on the other side.

Finally, a Samaritan came along. Samaritans and Jews did not usually get along. When he saw the man, instead of passing by, he felt

27

compassion for him, took care of his wounds with olive oil and wine, and bandaged him up. He put the man on his donkey and took him to an inn to care for him. The following day, the Samaritan gave the innkeeper two silver coins, and said, "Please care for this man. If his bill runs higher than this, I'll pay you the next time I'm here."

Jesus asked, "Which of these three men would you say was a good neighbor to the man who was attacked by bandits?"

The man who listened to the parable replied, "The one who showed him mercy."

"Yes!" Jesus said. "Now go and do the same." It didn't matter that the Samaritan and the Jew had different religions, different looks, or different social status. God calls us to help everyone in need because everyone is our neighbor.

Your Turn

1. Name a time you ignored someone who needed help, or a time you needed help and were ignored. How did it make you feel?

2. How can you be like the Good Samaritan and show compassion and mercy to others?

Do It!

Just as the Good Samaritan helped the injured man, you too can put others before yourself. Bake these delicious snickerdoodle cookies and consider how you can bring joy to someone's life.

Snickerdoodle Cookies

WHaT YOU NeeD

- 1½ cups sugar
- ½ cup softened butter
- ½ cup shortening
- 2 large eggs
- 2¾ cups all-purpose flour
- 2 teaspoons cream of tartar
- 1 teaspoon baking soda
- ¼ teaspoon salt
- 3 tablespoons sugar
- 3 teaspoons cinnamon
- cookie sheet

WHAT YOU DO

1. Preheat oven to 400°F.

2. Mix together 1½ cups sugar, butter, shortening, and eggs in a large bowl. Add in the flour, cream of tartar, baking soda and salt.

3. Chill dough in the refrigerator for 15 minutes.

4. Meanwhile, mix 3 tablespoons sugar, and 3 teaspoons cinnamon in a small bowl.

5. Shape dough into 1-inch balls, and then roll in cinnamon-sugar mixture. Place 2 inches apart on ungreased cookie sheet.

6. Bake 8 to 10 minutes. Remove from cookie sheet and place on a wire rack to cool.

7. Place cookies in a basket or container and give them away!

Bible Story

THe GOOD samaritan

Luke 10:25-37

Find the Missing Word

The Samaritan showed ____ ____ ____ ____ ____.

♡2

Write about It

The Bible tells us to not only look out for our own interests, but to bring joy into other people's lives as well. Use the space below to write (or doodle) about a time you put someone else first.

Tiny Treasure

When we are considerate of others, we are showing God's love.

Prayer

Lord God, thank you for giving me the Holy Spirit. Help me to put others first. In Jesus' name, amen.

(Hint: This is another word for "compassion," and it starts with an *m*.)

DON'T WORRY ABOUT ANYTHING

Turn all your worries over to him. He cares about you.

1 PETER 5:7

Emily's Fear

UGH! Another wrong note.

Emily inhaled and poised her fingers once again over the piano keys. Would she be able to perform the song flawlessly at Saturday's piano recital? That's what it would take to be a part of Miss Forte's Treble Clef Society.

"Play it again," Mrs. Emerson said, her hand directing in time with the metronome.

Emily started Chopin's "Waltz in A Minor" from the beginning. Her right hand was on autopilot, while her left fought to keep up. Emily let out a puff of air and continued playing, fumbling over the notes once again. If she kept making mistakes, would Mrs. Emerson give her something easier to play?

Unless she suddenly got sick . . .

"Emily, you're not concentrating," Mrs. Emerson said, pulling her back to the present. "You seem a million miles away." Mrs. Emerson continued.

"I know this song is difficult, but I wouldn't have given it to you if I didn't think you could do it. You've told me how much you want to join Miss Forte's piano society, and this piece will definitely help you meet your goal."

Emily blinked back tears. Her wish to join the Treble Clef Society had come back to haunt her. "I'm scared," she admitted.

"A few butterflies are okay," Mrs. Emerson said. "But too many nerves will stop you from being your best."

"Do you really think I can play this song by Saturday?"

"Yes." Mrs. Emerson nodded. "Do you?"

Emily shrugged. "My right hand knows what to do, but my left is having trouble."

"Let's work on that. I'll play the notes on the treble clef while you play the ones on the bass clef."

After more practice, Emily started to get the hang of it, but would she be able to play the song with both hands by Saturday?

Later, Emily wrote in her journal.

Dear God,

Guess what? By the end of my piano lesson, I played the whole song! No, it wasn't perfect, but at least my left hand could keep up with my right. Mrs. Emerson said if I practiced all week, she was positive I'd do a great job on Saturday. I sure hope so. Getting into Miss Forte's Treble Clef Society has been my dream for as long as I can remember. All I know is that when I tell you about my fears, I feel a whole lot better.

Love,

Emily

Your Turn

1. Do you play a musical instrument? Take photographs? Draw or paint? Write stories or poems? Write about your creative hobbies here.

2. Describe an experience when you wanted to be perfect to please someone.

3. Write about a time you prayed to God about your worries. How did it make you feel?

Did You Know?

When we worry, we are not trusting God with our lives. It is easy to forget God is in control when the world seems so out of control! But guess what? The Bible tells us not to worry.

Matthew 6:31–34 says,

> *So don't worry. Don't say, "What will we eat?" Or, "What will we drink?" Or, "What will we wear?" People who are ungodly run after all those things. Your Father who is in heaven knows that you need them. But put God's kingdom first. Do what he wants you to do. Then all those things will also be given to you. So don't worry about tomorrow. Tomorrow will worry about itself. Each day has enough trouble of its own."*

Try This!

Are you a worrywart? If you find yourself asking "what-if" questions, then you may be a worrywart. You know you're a worrywart if you constantly find yourself asking questions like, *What if Dad is late? What if my best friend moves away? What if a big, hairy spider crawls up my leg?* Yes, it's easy to worry, but remember God loves you and you can trust him.

Below are some simple tips to help you stop worrying:

1. Pray! God cares about you and wants you to give all your worries to him. Psalm 56:3 says, "When I am afraid, I put my trust in you."

2. Remember most of the things you worry about never happen.

3. Ask yourself, "What is the worst thing that can happen?" Then have a plan in place to put your mind at ease.

4. Don't think about scary things when you are hungry or tired. They appear bigger.

5. If you're worried about a relationship with a friend or family member, try not to guess what they are thinking. Talk it out.

6. Get exercise! It helps your body and your mind.

7. Tell a parent or trusted adult about your worries.

8. Relax! Read a book or go outside and enjoy nature. Use all five senses—hear, see, touch, smell, and taste (if appropriate).

9. Take a small step to conquer your fear. Remember, before you get good at anything, you need to practice!

Be sure to try them all, but choose your favorite and make it into a poster. Print the tip on a large sheet of paper and then add drawings, stickers, or other decorations. Hang your worry-free poster in a place you will see it every day.

Do It!

Scrambled Senses

Unscramble these words to see how you can use your five senses to put aside your worries. Next, fill in the blank with the correct word to complete each Bible verse.

1. *You can see the snow-capped*

   ___ ___ ___ ___ ___ ___ ___ ___ ___ (UOISNNaTM)

   "The _____ might shake. The hills might be removed. But my faithful love for you will never be shaken. And my covenant that promises peace to you will never be removed," says the LORD. He shows you his loving concern. Isaiah 54:10

2. *You can hear the* ___ ___ ___ ___ (NIDW) *rustling the*
   ___ ___ ___ ___ ___ ___ (VLeeSa) *on the* ___ ___ ___ ___ ___ (reSeT).

   [Jesus] got up and ordered the _____ to stop. He said to the waves, "Quiet! Be still!" Then the _____ died down. And it was completely calm. Mark 4:39

3. *You can smell the beautiful* ___ ___ ___ ___ ___ ___ ___ (WreFOSL).

   The grass dries up. The _____ fall to the ground. But what our God says will stand forever. Isaiah 40:8

4. *You can* ___ ___ ___ ___ ___ (eSTaT) *an apple from an apple tree.*

   _____ *and see that the LORD is good. Blessed is the person who goes to him for safety. Psalm 34:8*

5. *You can touch the cool ocean* ___ ___ ___ ___ ___ (TaWre) *or the*

6. ___ ___ ___ ___ ___ (SraGS) *beneath bare feet.*

   Jesus stood up and spoke in a loud voice. He said, "Let anyone who is thirsty come to me and drink. Does anyone believe in me? Then, just as Scripture says, rivers of living _____ will flow from inside them." When he said this, he meant the Holy Spirit. John 7:37–39

Answer key on page 166.

I was very worried. But your comfort brought me joy.

PSALM 94:19

Bible Story

THE WIDOW AT ZAREPHATH

1 Kings 17:8-24

The Lord said to Elijah, "Go and live in the village of Zarephath, near the city of Sidon. I have instructed a widow there to care for you."

So Elijah did as God asked. He went to Zarephath and arrived at the gates of the village. He saw the widow gathering sticks, and he asked her, "Would you please bring me a cup of water? And a bite to eat, too?"

However, the widow replied, "I don't have a single piece of bread in the house. All I have is a handful of flour and a little cooking oil. I was just gathering a few sticks to cook our last meal. After we eat it, my son and I will die."

Then Elijah said to her, "Do not be afraid! Go and make bread for me first, then use what is left to prepare a meal for yourself and your son. For the Lord God of Israel says

39

that there will always be flour left in the jar and cooking oil in the bottom of the jug until he sends rain and the crops grow again!"

So the widow did as Elijah said, and Elijah and her family continued to eat for many days. There was always enough flour and olive oil left in the containers, just as the Lord had promised.

Sometime later, the widow's son became sick. He grew worse and worse until finally he died. The widow said to Elijah, "O man of God, what have you done to me? Have you come to show me my sins and kill my son?"

Elijah replied, "Give me your son." He took the boy from her arms and carried him up the stairs to the room where he was staying, and laid the body on his bed. Elijah cried out to God, "O Lord my God, why have you brought tragedy to this widow who has opened her home to me, causing her son to die? O Lord, please let this child's life return to him."

God heard Elijah's prayer, and the boy came back to life!

Then Elijah brought the boy down from the upper room and gave him to his mother. "Look!" he said, "Your son is alive!"

The widow said to Elijah, "Now I know you are a man of God, and that the Lord truly speaks through you."

Your Turn

1. How did the widow take care of Elijah even though she was worried?

2. What did Elijah do to show the widow that God loves and cares for her?

Do It!

Just as God provided flour and cooking oil for the widow and Elijah, the Lord will also take care of you! Create this keepsake craft to remind you how much God loves you.

Clay Flower Thumbprint Keepsake

WHAT YOU NEED

- 2 cups flour
- 1 cup salt
- 2 tablespoon vegetable oil
- ¾ cup water
- bowl and spatula for mixing
- plastic plate
- toothpicks
- pencil
- baking parchment paper and cooking sheet
- water-based acrylic paints and paintbrush
- large buttons
- craft glue
- ribbon

WHAT YOU DO

1. With adult supervision, preheat oven to 250°F.

2. In a bowl, mix the flour and salt.

3. Add the vegetable oil, and then slowly add the water. Knead with your hands until it is smooth and stretchy. If it feels too sticky, add a touch more flour. If it is too dry and crumbly, add a bit more water.

4. Flatten the clay ball onto a plastic plate and shape into a circle or heart.

42

5. In a circular fashion, make a flower design on the clay by pressing your thumb five times per flower to create petals, leaving room to place buttons in the center.

6. Use a pencil to add holes to the top so that you can hang your creation after baking.

7. With a toothpick, write a saying, such as God cares for me on your plaque. Or add your name and birth date.

8. Carefully transfer the clay to baking parchment paper and a cookie sheet, and bake the clay for 1 hour. Note: If your clay is thick, bake at 100°F for 3 hours to prevent cracking.

9. Let cool. Glue buttons to the center of the flowers. Paint as much or as little as you like. Let dry.

10. Add ribbon or string through the holes to hang.

Enjoy yourself or give as a gift.

Bible Story

THE WIDOW AT ZarePHaTH

1 Kings 17:8-24

Find the Missing Word

God heard ___ ___ ___ ___ ___ ___'s prayer.

♡3

Write about It

Above all, God desires us to seek him first. Use the space below to write (or doodle) about a time God helped you conquer your fear and brought you joy.

Tiny Treasure

Worrying doesn't add a single moment to your life. If God helps flowers grow, he will definitely take care of you!

Prayer

Lord God, thank you for hearing my prayers. Help me to have joy in my heart instead of fear. In Jesus' name, amen.

Pray About Everything

> *Always be joyful. Never stop praying.*
> *Give thanks no matter what happens. God wants*
> *you to thank him because you believe in Christ Jesus.*
>
> 1 THESSALONIANS 5:16–18

Jessica's Prayer

Jessica's knees wobbled as she stood in front of the entire school for the spelling bee. Only two students sat in chairs behind her. The grand prize was a $100 shopping spree and a cupcake party, as well as the possibility to move on to the county and state competitions. Jessica had dreamed of winning the spelling bee since she was in second grade, and had prayed about it every year since.

"Lackadaisical," Mrs. Anderson, the English teacher, said.

"Lackadaisical. May I have the definition, please?" Jessica asked.

"Lacking enthusiasm and determination; carelessly lazy. Lackadaisical."

"Lackadaisical. L-A-C-K-A-D-A-I-S-I-C-A-L. Lackadaisical."

"That is correct." Mrs. Anderson nodded. Thank goodness Jessica had practiced! She breathed a sigh of relief.

Jessica glanced to Chloe on her right. She wasn't getting up to go to the microphone. "Psst. It's your turn," Jessica whispered.

"I feel sick," Chloe whispered. She hesitated a few more seconds before making her way to the microphone.

Jessica was so wrapped up in her own thoughts, she couldn't focus on what was happening. The next thing she knew, she heard Mrs. Anderson say, "I'm sorry. That is incorrect."

Chloe ran off the stage and through the gym doors. Maybe she was sick after all! Now it was down to Jessica and Alex. If either of them misspelled their word, the other person would have to spell two words correctly to win! Alex approached the microphone for his word.

"Indomitable," Mrs. Anderson said.

"Indomitable." Alex's voice cracked. "Can I have the definition?"

"Impossible to subdue or defeat. Indomitable."

"Indomitable. I-N-D-O-M-I-T-I-B-L-E. Indomitable."

"I'm sorry, that is incorrect." Mrs. Anderson shook her head. Alex shuffled to his seat. If Jessica spelled the next two words correctly, she'd win! Her prayers would be answered. She made her way to the microphone.

Later that night, Jessica wrote in her journal.

> **Dear God,**
>
> **I WON THE SPELLING BEE!!! WHOO HOO! YIPPEE!** Alex was such a good sport. He shook my hand and told me that I was tough competition. I asked Alex and Chloe if they wanted to join me for the cupcake party. At first they looked shocked. Truthfully, any one of us could have won, so why not share the prize? Thank you for listening to all my prayers about the spelling bee.
>
> **Love,**
>
> **Jessica**

Your Turn

1. Describe a time you were in a competition. Did you win? Write about it here.

2. Name something you have prayed for a very long time. Did you get what you asked for? How did you feel?

3. How can you stay thankful while you wait for God to answer your prayers?

Did You Know?

God doesn't always say yes to our prayers. Sometimes his answer is no and other times it is to wait. The truth is, God knows what we need when we need it. But waiting can be hard!

The good news is that during those times of waiting we learn how to be patient, which grows our faith. When we wait patiently for God to answer our prayers, it shows that we love Jesus and put our trust in him. By honoring God in this way, we encourage others to do the same.

Try This!

While you wait for God to answer your prayers, think about these verses:

- *Be strong and brave . . . The Lord your God will go with you. He will never leave you. He'll never desert you* (Deuteronomy 31:6).

- *God is able to do far more than we could ever ask for or imagine. He does everything by his power that is working in us* (Ephesians 3:20).

- *We know that in all things God works for the good of those who love him. He appointed them to be saved in keeping with his purpose* (Romans 8:28).

Try singing the words of one of these verses to a simple tune like "Mary Had a Little Lamb," "Row, Row, Row Your Boat," or "London Bridge." Learning verses to well known tunes is a great way to memorize them. And these are great verses to memorize so you can remember when times are tough.

Consider these five things while you wait for God to answer your prayer:

1. Remember what God has done for you in the past.
2. Read your Bible to learn more about God.
3. Ask God to forgive you for your sins.
4. Dream big, knowing God can accomplish anything, and then trust him.
5. Sing worship songs and praise God for what he has already done in your life.

Do It!

*When you pray, go into your room. Close the door and pray to
your Father, who can't be seen. Your Father will reward you,
because he sees what you do secretly.* Matthew 6:6

In Matthew 6:9–13, we read about the time Jesus taught his disciples how to pray.

Find the hidden words of the Lord's Prayer in this word search, and
remember that praying to God is like talking with your best friend.

Lord's Prayer Word Search

```
Y  M  M  F  O  r  G  I  V  e  W  T  O  D  a  Y  a  Y
K  N  T  F  Y  B  a  H  e  a  V  e  N  Z  Z  B  P  U
Z  T  Q  S  D  K  a  G  T  B  K  G  I  V  e  N  T  K
T  e  F  a  D  a  I  a  a  P  Q  K  Y  H  K  S  C  I
H  M  O  V  H  G  I  V  H  I  K  e  e  P  K  I  H  N
D  P  r  e  a  O  O  L  K  M  N  Q  X  B  r  N  a  G
O  T  G  K  W  a  N  T  Y  V  V  S  r  B  C  S  P  D
N  e  I  Y  G  H  B  O  B  I  N  N  T  I  D  I  P  O
e  D  V  e  a  r  T  H  r  Y  F  a  T  H  e  r  e  M
D  W  e  P  D  K  r  a  K  e  Y  M  T  Z  Q  G  N  e
H  Y  N  W  Z  K  Y  r  S  H  D  e  B  r  e  a  D  e
S  G  W  r  r  K  O  M  e  V  I  L  U  S  r  G  a  V
```

Against	*Earth*	*Forgiven*	*Honored*	*Save*	*Us*
Bread	*Evil*	*Give*	*Keep*	*Sins*	*Want*
Daily	*Father*	*Happen*	*Kingdom*	*Tempted*	
Done	*Forgive*	*Heaven*	*Name*	*Today*	

Answer key on page 166.

When you hope, be joyful. When you suffer, be patient. When you pray, be faithful.

romans 12:12

Bible Story

Hannah's request

1 Samuel 1:2-20, 24-28

Elkanah had two wives, Hannah and Peninnah. Peninnah had children, but Hannah did not. Each year Elkanah would travel to Shiloh to worship at the Tabernacle. On the days Elkanah presented his sacrifice, he would give portions of the meat to Peninnah and each of her children. And though he loved Hannah, he would give her only one choice portion because the Lord had given her no children.

So Peninnah would mock Hannah and make fun of her because the Lord had kept her from having children. Year after year it was the same—Peninnah would tease Hannah as they went to the Tabernacle. Each time, Hannah would cry and not eat.

"Hannah, why are you crying?" Elkanah would ask, "Why aren't you eating? Why be sad just because you have no children? You have me—isn't that better than having ten sons?"

Once after a sacrificial meal at Shiloh, Hannah got up and went to pray. Eli the priest was sitting at his customary place beside the entrance of the Tabernacle. Hannah was in deep anguish, crying bitterly as she prayed to the Lord. And she made this vow: "Lord, if you will look upon my sorrow and answer my prayer and give me a son, then I will give him back to you. He will be yours for his entire lifetime, and as a sign that he has been dedicated to the Lord, his hair will never be cut."

As she was praying to the Lord, Eli watched her. Seeing her lips moving

but hearing no sound, he thought she had been drinking. "Must you come here drunk?" he demanded. "Throw away your wine!"

"Oh no, sir!" she replied. "I haven't been drinking wine or anything stronger. But I am very discouraged, and I was pouring out my heart to the Lord. Don't think I am a wicked woman! For I have been praying out of great anguish and sorrow."

"In that case," Eli said, "go in peace! May the God of Israel grant the request you have asked of him."

"Oh, thank you, sir!" she exclaimed. Then she went back and began to eat again, and was no longer sad.

The entire family got up early the next morning and went to worship the Lord once more. Then they returned home to Ramah. The Lord remembered Hannah's plea, and in due time she gave birth to a son. She named him Samuel, for she said, "I asked the Lord for him."

When the boy was old enough, Hannah took him to Eli and said, "Sir do you remember me? I am the very woman who stood here several years ago praying to the Lord. I asked the Lord to give me this boy. God has granted my request, as you said. Now I am giving him to the Lord, and he will belong to the Lord his whole life."

Your Turn

1. Why did Hannah pray for a son? How did God answer her prayer?

2. Write about a time you made a promise to God if he would give you what you asked for.

Do It!

Just as Hannah prayed for a child, you too can ask God for whatever is on your heart. Create this gratitude journal and consider how you can be thankful in all circumstances.

Paper Bag Gratitude Journal

WHAT YOU NEED

- 3 paper lunch bags
- hole punch
- pencil
- 3 pieces of ribbon or string 4- to 6-inches long
- colorful napkin or markers
- glue
- colored paper
- scissors

WHAT YOU DO

1. Stack the folded paper bags on top of each other with the openings together and fold in half to create the book.

2. Punch three holes on the folded side of one bag. Using this bag's holes as a guide, use pencil to mark where to punch holes in the other two bags. When holes have been punched in all three bags, sandwich them together and make sure the holes line up.

3. Thread a length of ribbon or string through each hole and tie to secure.

4. Fully open a colorful napkin and cut out one of the squares. Glue to the front of the gratitude journal. Or create your own design on the front of your journal using markers.

5. Write or draw what you are thankful for inside your gratitude journal.

alternate idea

A paper bag journal has fun pockets. Cut out colorful pieces of paper and write what you are thankful for on each one. Tuck them inside the pockets. At the end of the month, pull out the papers and read what you wrote. You will be amazed at how God has blessed you.

Bible Story

HaNNaH'S reQUeST

1 Samuel 1:2-20, 24-27

Find the Missing Word

Hannah prayed to the ___ ___ ___ ___.

Write about It

God wants us to always be joyful and never stop praying. Use the space below to write (or doodle) about something you are praying for right now!

Tiny Treasure

God knows us better than we know ourselves, and we can trust him to answer our prayers.

Prayer

Lord God, thank you for hearing my prayers. Help me to be grateful while I wait on you. In Jesus' name, amen.

WHAT IS TRUE

Truthful words last forever.
But lies last for only a moment.
PROVERBS 12:19

Lauren's Lies

Why did she open her big mouth? Lauren stood among the group of girls, wishing she hadn't told them she liked the new sci-fi movie everyone was talking about. She hadn't even seen it! Emma nudged her with an elbow. "Lauren, what was your favorite part?"

"Well . . . I liked the ending, but I had to use the restroom and missed part of it." Another lie!

During recess, several girls did each other's hair in French braids. Emma offered to braid Lauren's hair, too. Instead of simply saying she didn't want her hair that way, Lauren sat patiently while Emma stood behind her grabbing, pulling, and twisting it into the braid.

At lunch, Emma handed Lauren a note. It said:

> **You didn't say anything about my new shoes. Do you like them?**
>
> **Yes   No**

If Lauren circled "Yes," she would be lying. And if she circled "No," Emma's feelings would be hurt. Lauren couldn't win either way.

An idea struck. She reached inside her backpack, snagged
a pen, and circled the word "Yes," then wrote:

> They are a very pretty color! I LOVE blue.

Lauren handed the note back to Emma before the bell rang.

"You really like them?" Emma asked, staring down at her shoes. "I think
they're ugly, but I didn't want to hurt my mom's feelings. She bought
them on sale and can't return them, so I have to make the best of it."

The urge to tell Emma the complete truth about everything that happened
swelled inside. "I've never watched the sci-fi movie, I don't like my hair in a
French braid, and I think your shoes are ugly." Lauren let out a deep breath.

Emma's face turned five different shades of red before she grabbed her stomach,
tilted her head back . . . and laughed! Lauren couldn't help but laugh, too.

Later that night, Lauren wrote in her journal.

> Dear God,
>
> Telling lies (even small ones) is exhausting! The truth is always much
> better. I'm so glad Emma didn't get mad at me. Can you believe she
> laughed? She said I have to tell the rest of the girls that I didn't
> watch the sci-fi movie. (Looks creepy!) My friends might think I'm
> a baby, but everyone has their own likes and dislikes, right?
>
> Love,
>
> Lauren

Your Turn

1. Describe a time you told a lie. How did it make you feel?

2. Write about a time when you told a fib just to be nice to someone.

3. Why is it wrong to tell a lie to make someone feel good?

Did You Know?

Satan is the father of lies. John 8:44 says that Satan "has never obeyed the truth. There is no truth in him. When he lies, he speaks his natural language. He does this because he is a liar. He is the father of lies."

Webster's dictionary defines *truth* as "the state of being the case: fact." In the Bible, Jesus says, "I am the way and the truth and the life. No one comes to the Father except through me" (John 14:6).

What does that really mean? Jesus is the truth. He is God. In order to spend eternity with our Father in Heaven, we need to believe Jesus died for our sins, confess our sins, and follow him. John 3:16 says, "God so loved the world that he gave his one and only Son. Anyone who believes in him will not die but will have eternal life."

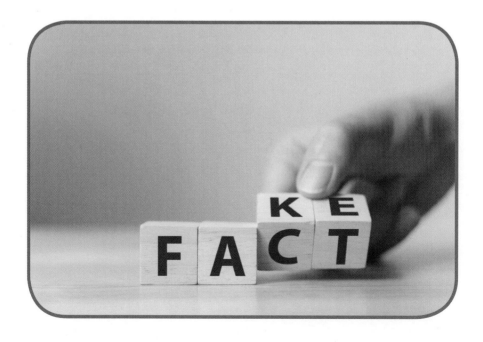

Try This!

You can find true joy by speaking the truth instead of telling lies, and believing in the truth—which is Jesus Christ! When you follow Jesus, you will want to speak the truth no matter how difficult it may be.

Below are seven steps to help you tell the truth. Some of the words are written backwards. On the lines provided, print the word correctly.

1. daeR _____ the elbiB _____. You can discover what God thinks is important in his Word, the Bible.

2. yarP_____! Ask God to help you tell the truth at all times.

3. Ask snoitseuq _____. If you want to know why others think the way they do, ask. You may or may not agree with them, but it will help you discover your feelings.

4. Be tsenoh _____. In order to tell the truth, you need to be honest with yourself and others. Don't be afraid to share your feelings instead of going along with the crowd.

5. Write down your sgnileef _____ in a journal. Tell God exactly what is on your mind.

6. kaepS _____ the hturt _____ in evol _____. Being truthful doesn't mean that you purposely hurt someone's feelings. Remember to be kind and gentle. When you speak the truth in love, you are becoming more like Jesus (Ephesians 4:15).

7. If you are still having a difficult time telling the truth, klat _____ with an tluda _____ and ask for advice.

Do It!

Truth Maze

Learning to always tell the truth can feel like walking through a maze. It may be hard at first, but once you commit your life to God it will get easier. Grab a pencil, and start at the opening at the top and weave your way to the middle without crossing any lines. Along the correct path, you'll find the words of the verse. Write them in order on the blank lines below.

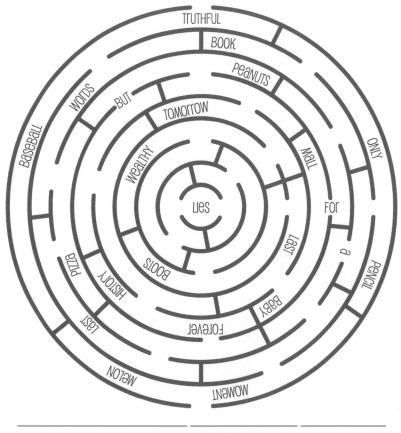

_____ _____ _____

_____. _____ _____ _____

_____ _____ ____ _____ (Proverbs 12:19).

Answer key on page 166.

Instead, we will speak the truth in love. So we will grow up in every way to become the body of Christ. Christ is the head of the body.

ephesians 4:15

Bible Story

Jacob Steals Esau's Blessing

Genesis 27

Isaac, who had grown old and blind, called for his firstborn son, Esau.

"I don't know when I may die," Isaac said. "Go hunt some wild game and prepare some tasty food for me. Then, I will give you my blessing to inherit everything I own when I die."

Rebekah, Isaac's wife, overheard what Isaac had said. She wanted her younger son Jacob to receive the blessing instead of Esau. When Esau left to hunt, she told Jacob, "Go out to the flocks, and bring me two fine young goats. I'll prepare your father's favorite dish. Take the food to your father so he can eat it and bless you before he dies."

Jacob went out and got the goats for his mother. Rebekah took them and prepared a delicious meal, just the way Isaac liked it. Then she took Esau's clothes and gave them to Jacob. She covered his arms and neck with the skin of the young goats, because Esau was covered with hair while Jacob had smooth skin.

Jacob took the food to his father. "Father?" he said.

Isaac answered. "Are you Esau or Jacob?"

Jacob replied, "It's Esau, your firstborn son. I've done as you told me. Here is the food I prepared."

Isaac asked, "How did you find it so quickly, my son?"

"God helped me," Jacob lied.

"Come closer so I can touch you," Isaac said. So Jacob went closer to his father, and Isaac touched him. "The voice is Jacob's, but the hands are hairy like Esau's. Are you really my son Esau?"

"Yes, I am," Jacob lied again.

Jacob took the food to his father, and Isaac ate it. Then Isaac said to Jacob, "Please come a little closer."

When Isaac caught the smell of Esau's clothes, he blessed Jacob.

Meanwhile, Esau returned from his hunt, prepared a delicious meal, and brought it to his father. Then he said, "Eat my wild game, father, so you can give me your blessing."

But Isaac asked him, "Who are you?"

Esau replied, "It's your firstborn son, Esau."

Isaac began to tremble uncontrollably. "Your brother was here, and he tricked me. He has taken away your blessing!"

Esau broke down and wept. When he was done weeping, he became very angry and bitter toward Jacob for his greedy trick. He even wanted to kill Jacob! Rebekah sent Jacob away so he would be safe from Esau's anger.

Your Turn

1. Why did Jacob lie to his father?

2. Why is it always better to tell the truth?

Do It!

Just as Jacob stole the blessing from his brother Esau, you can hurt those around you if you lie. Create this snack and consider the importance of telling the truth.

Apple Peanut Butter Smile

WHAT YOU NEED

- 1 red apple
- Apple slicer (or use knife)
- Knife
- ¼ to ½ cup of peanut butter (or an alternative like sunflower seed butter if you are allergic)
- Mini-marshmallows

WHAT YOU DO

1. With adult supervision, core and slice the apple with an apple slicer or knife. You will need two apple slices per mouth.

2. Use knife to spread a layer of peanut butter on one side of each slice.

3. Line a row of marshmallows across the peanut butter on half of the apple slices to look like teeth.

4. Place second peanut butter slathered apple slice on top to form a big-toothed smile.

5. Enjoy!

Bible Story

JaCOB STeaLS eSaU'S BLeSSING

Genesis 27

Find the Missing Word

Rebekah told Jacob to bring her two fine ___ ___ ___ ___ ___ goats.

Write about It

Use the space below to write (or doodle) about a time
God helped you speak the truth in love.

Tiny Treasure

True joy is found in Jesus! He will help you tell the truth.

Prayer

Lord God, thank you for Jesus and for eternal life. Help me
to speak the truth at all times. In Jesus' name, amen.

WHaT IS HONOraBLE

Don't pay back evil with evil. Be careful to do what everyone thinks is right.

ROMaNS 12:17

Savannah's Choice

Life was strange now that Savannah's parents were separated. Dad lived in an apartment a few blocks away, and every Monday night her parents went to counseling, leaving Savannah home alone.

On one of those Monday nights, Savannah walked to the pantry and pulled out a toaster pastry. The hardwood floor creaked beneath her feet. Besides the creaky floors, the house made other strange noises and it was dark outside. Her heart pounded. *Why don't these things bother me when Mom's home?*

She hurried to her bedroom and climbed on top of her bed.

BOOM! A loud crash sounded outside her window.

Savannah yelped and dove under the covers. *It's just a raccoon in the trash cans,* she tried to convince herself. Steeling her nerves, she got up, went to the window and peeked out. From the glow of the streetlamp, she saw two kids wearing hooded sweatshirts running down the street. Savannah recognized the orange lava goo on the right shoulder of Ethan's sweatshirt. The other kid must be Jacob, his best friend.

Ethan must still be mad at her for ruining his volcano. She'd

apologized and thought he was over it by now. "Guess not!" she sputtered aloud. Savannah pulled the curtains shut. She thought about how she could get back at Ethan and Jacob for scaring her.

She could put something disgusting in their backpacks.

She could write a nasty note about them and pass it around school.

Or she could call the police! They were trespassing, after all.

Savannah paced back and forth until she heard the garage door open and her mom walk in.

"What have you been up to tonight?" Mom asked.

Could she tell her mom how scared she'd been? How Ethan and Jacob had pranked her, making her even more afraid? Instead, Savannah asked, "How's Dad?"

"Good, I guess." Mom shrugged. "We're working on our communication skills."

Ever since her parents separated, her mom had promised not to say anything bad about her father. No matter what he did, she would never pay back "evil for evil." Whatever that meant.

Later that night, Savannah wrote in her journal.

> **Dear God,**
>
> **Mom says that it's better to have integrity than to get back at someone. In other words, to be honorable. Although it would be fun to put rubber snakes in Ethan and Jacob's backpacks or tape a "Kick me" sign to their backs, for now, I'll resist!**
>
> **Love,**
>
> **Savannah**

Your Turn

1. Describe a time someone was mean to you. How did that experience make you feel?

2. Did you get back at them, or did you choose to be honorable? What would you do if it happened again?

Did You Know?

Respect is another word for *honor*. Romans 12:10 says, "Love one another deeply. Honor others more than yourselves."

The Bible says we are to honor our parents (Ephesians 6:2), older people (Leviticus 19:32), and those in authority, such as your teachers, your pastor, or those in government (Romans 13:1). However, the ultimate authority and honor belong to God because he is the one who created us.

1 Chronicles 29:11 says, "Lord, you are great and powerful. Glory, majesty and beauty belong to you. Everything in heaven and on earth belongs to you. Lord, the kingdom belongs to you. You are honored as the one who rules over all."

Another way we can honor God is by believing in his Son, Jesus Christ, who died on the cross for your sins, resurrected from the dead, and ascended into Heaven.

Try This!

Below are ten ways to show honor to God and others:

1. Use the talents God gave you.
2. Praise God by singing songs, listening to worship music, or playing an instrument.
3. Speak respectfully to your parents.
4. Be quiet in class when your teacher is talking.
5. Listen to your coach.
6. Open a door for an older person.
7. Read the Bible and books about him (like this one!).
8. Write a thank-you note when you receive a gift.
9. Tell people you appreciate them.
10. Pray for a friend.

Probably the best way to honor God is by telling others the story of when you decided to follow Jesus. If they ask questions, you may not know the answers, but that's OK! God doesn't expect you to know everything. He just wants you to share about what you've seen him do in your life.

Practice what you might say by writing two or three sentences about your decision to follow Jesus.

_____

_____

_____

_____

_____

_____

_____

_____

Do It!

You can honor God and others by the decisions you make. Just as Savannah chose not to get back at Ethan and Jacob, with God's help you can make good decisions, too.

Decision Quiz

1. Your sibling took the last slice of pizza even though your mom said you can have it. Do you:

   a. Grab the pizza from her hand and eat it. After all, your mom said it was yours.

   B. Ask her to split it with you.

   C. Tell her she can have it. There is always next time.

2. Your best friend invited you over for a sleepover, and then cancelled at the last minute. Do you:

   a. Tell your friend you are coming anyway, and then apologize.

   B. Call her and ask if everything is all right. There must have been a good reason she cancelled.

   C. Spy on her to see if she invited someone else and think of ways you can spoil her night.

3. Your dad is leaving again for another business trip. Do you:

   a. Tuck a note in his briefcase, telling him how much you love him.

   B. Complain that he is always gone.

   C. Give your dad the silent treatment, and then hug him before he leaves.

4. Your soccer coach always makes you do exercises before you scrimmage. Do you:

   a. Tell him you have a stomachache so that you can skip the exercises.

   B. Give it your best effort so that you'll be in tip-top shape.

   C. Only do your best when the coach is looking.

5. Your teacher is teaching a math lesson to the class. Do you:

   a. Lay your head on your desk and take a nap.

   B. Think about other things for a while, before paying attention.

   C. Listen the entire time so that you'll know how to do your homework.

Answer key on page 166.

Is anyone among you wise and understanding? That person should show it by living a good life. A wise person isn't proud when they do good deeds.

JAMES 3:13

Bible Story

DAVID SPARES SAUL'S LIFE

1 Samuel 24:1-22

God had said that David would be king. And that made Saul—who was the king—really mad. King Saul was so jealous of David that he took 3,000 men with him into the desert to find and kill David.

One day during the search for David, Saul entered a cave to relieve himself. But as it happened, David and his men were hiding farther back in that very same cave!

"Now's your chance!" David's men whispered to him. They thought David should kill Saul before Saul killed him! But David didn't hate Saul. Instead, David crept forward and cut off a piece of Saul's robe.

David's conscience bothered him for cutting Saul's robe. He said to his men, "I shouldn't attack the Lord's anointed one, for the Lord himself has chosen him." David would not let his men kill Saul.

After Saul had left the cave, David came out and shouted after him, "My Lord the king!" And when Saul looked around, David bowed low before him.

Then he shouted to Saul,

> Why do you listen when people say I am trying to harm you? It isn't true. When you were in the cave, some of my men told me to kill you, but instead I spared your life. For I said, "I will never harm the king—he is the Lord's anointed one." Look at what I have in my hand. It is a piece of the hem of your robe! I cut it off, but I didn't kill you. This proves that I am not trying to harm you and that I have not sinned against you, even though you have been hunting for me to kill me.

When David had finished speaking, Saul called back, "Is that really you, David?" Then he began to cry. And he said to David,

> You are a better man than I. You have repaid me good for evil. When the Lord put me in a place where you could have killed me, you didn't do it. May the Lord reward you well for your kindness.

> And now I realize that you are surely going to be king, and that the kingdom of Israel will flourish under your rule. Give me your word that you will not kill my family and destroy my line of descendants!

David made the promise. Then Saul went home, but David and his men went back to their stronghold.

Your Turn

1. What choice did David make in the cave? Why did he make that choice?

2. What can help you choose good over evil in difficult situations?

3. Are you facing a difficult situation now? If so, how can you choose to do good instead of evil?

Do It!

You can be like David and chose good over evil, making wise decisions. Create this bracelet to remind you to live an honorable life.

Craft Stick Bracelets

What You Need

- Jumbo craft sticks
- Shallow dish
- Water, boiling
- Large spoon
- Mug or drinking glass
- Fingernail file
- Colored markers
- Decorations (faux jewels, sequins, glitter, scrapbooking paper, fabric, decorative tape, duct tape, etc.)
- Paintbrush
- Decoupage medium (Mod Podge, white glue and water, etc.)

What You Do

1. With adult supervision, place craft sticks in a shallow dish and cover with boiling water. Place a large spoon on top to weigh down the craft sticks (image a). Let sit for 30 minutes.

2. Repeat the first step at least two more times. You may want to leave them soaking in water overnight.

A

3. Slowly and very carefully bend each craft stick to fit it inside a mug (image b). (Don't worry if some sticks split or break. It's bound to happen!) Leave overnight to dry.

4. Remove the craft sticks from the drinking glass and file any rough edges.

5. Decorate your bracelets. Be creative!

6. Brush on a layer of decoupage medium to seal and let dry.

7. Enjoy!

B

ENRICHMENT IDEA

Before bending the craft sticks, ask an adult to help you drill a hole at each end. You can use a drill, awl, or wood burning tool to make the holes. Through each hole, attach a few inches of plastic or leather lacing or embroidery floss so you can tie the bracelet around your wrist.

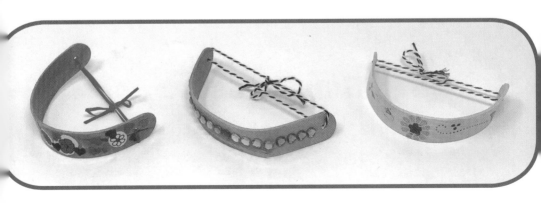

Bible Story

DaViD SPareS SauL'S LIFe

1 Samuel 24:1-22

Find the Missing Word

The Lord ___ ___ ___ ___ ___ ___ ___ David to kill Saul.

♡6

Write about It

When you live an honorable life, you want to do good and help others. Use the space below to write (or doodle) about a time you showed honor to someone.

Tiny Treasure

To understand God's ways, live an honorable life.

Prayer

Lord God, thank you for helping me make good choices instead of paying back evil for evil. Help me to honor you always. In Jesus' name, amen.

(Hint: This word means you're not allowed to do something and it starts with an *f*.)

WHaT IS rIGHT

Don't live the way this world lives.
Let your way of thinking be completely changed.
Then you will be able to test what God wants
for you. And you will agree that what he wants
is right. His plan is good and pleasing and perfect.

rOMaNS 12:2

Brianna's Behavior

"Yikes!" Brianna shrieked when she saw her friend, Hannah. "You have a bald spot on your head. What did you do? Get your hair caught in the curling iron or something?"

"About that . . ." Hannah covered the spot with her hand. "A couple of weeks ago the doctor told me I have an autoimmune disease called *alopecia*. My immune system is attacking my hair follicles. It's like my body is allergic to my own hair."

Brianna's eyes narrowed. "Are you going bald?"

Hannah shrugged. "If the creams and injections don't work, I might. I've decided to tell the whole school about my alopecia before someone sees my bald spot and makes fun of me."

That was a few days ago. Now as Brianna's mom drove her to school, she couldn't get what Hannah said out of her head. Truthfully, she didn't know if she could handle having a bald friend. It would be hard to go to the mall, the frozen yogurt shop, the movies, or anywhere else knowing people were whispering and pointing. It would be embarrassing!

Brianna's mom pulled the car up to the curb in front of the school. "Have a great day!" Mom said.

Brianna doubted that was possible. All morning she walked around school in a daze, waiting for the big reveal.

Then during lunch, the principal hushed the crowd. "Hannah Conroy, please come forward." Hannah had worn a thick headband, covering up the bald spot. Tears pricked Brianna's eyes.

The announcement went by in a blur as Hannah explained her condition, including the fact that there was no cure. The bald patches on her head would most likely grow wider.

At that moment Brianna realized she would always be Hannah's friend, bald or not! Yes, there would be hard moments watching her friend's hair fall out, but if Hannah could go through it with a positive attitude, so could Brianna.

As Hannah walked back to her seat, Brianna jumped to her feet and gave her friend a standing ovation.

Surprisingly, the entire student body stood and erupted in applause. Guess they were proud of Hannah, too!

That night, Brianna wrote in her journal.

Dear God,

Guess what? Mom researched online and found an organization that takes donated hair. Yep, I decided to donate twelve inches of my hair to help bald kids get a wig! Thank you for giving me the courage to do the right thing and stand by my friend.

Love,

Brianna

Your Turn

1. Describe a situation when you stood up for someone even though it seemed overwhelming at the time.

2. Name a time you made the right decision even though it was tough. How did it make you feel?

3. What is one thing you can do today to help someone in need?

Did You Know?

Some decisions are easy to make, while others are more difficult. Writing a list of pros and cons can help you decide which decision is best, but when it is a choice between right and wrong, it is always best to do the right thing!

But how do we know? One way is to search your Bible to find out what God says on the matter. He has given us clear direction on many things, such as the Ten Commandments (Exodus 20:1–17) and how he wants us to live our lives. God has also given us the Holy Spirit to guide us (John 14:26).

The following questions can help you determine the right thing to do:

1. What does the Bible say you should do?
2. What have your parents taught you to do?
3. What is your conscience telling you?
4. How will you feel about yourself later if you do it? How would you feel about yourself if you *didn't* do it?
5. How would you feel if someone did it to you?

Try This!

As you grow older, you will have more and more responsibilities, like driving a car or owning your own home, but that doesn't mean you shouldn't learn to be responsible now. By choosing to do the right thing and showing responsibility, you will gain your parents' trust and earn more freedom. Besides, being responsible shows that you respect yourself, as well as others.

The next page shows ten ways to become more responsible. Each time you do one of them, put a sticker or draw an X in a box next to the thing you did. See if you can get a bingo! Then go for a black-out bingo by filling in every square!

Take care of yourself and your belongings.					
Be on time.					
Follow through with your chores, homework, and other commitments.					
Set goals and work hard to achieve them.					
Admit when you make a mistake.					
Be trustworthy.					
Treat others as you would like to be treated.					
Think before you speak.					
Say "no" to peer pressure.					
Be true to yourself and your values.					

Do It!

Bravery Quiz

In order to do the right thing, you need to push your fears away and learn to be brave. How courageous would you be in each of these situations? Check the box of the answer that describes you.

You see a lost dog. You . . .

☐ Ignore it and keep walking.
☐ Ask an adult to help you find the owner.

Your friend is mean to someone at school. You . . .

☐ Talk to your friend and encourage her to be nice.
☐ Laugh along even though you know it is hurting the person's feelings.

The girl sitting beside you wants you to help her cheat on a test. You . . .

☐ Put your paper close enough for her to see it.
☐ Cover your paper with your hand.

A group of your friends want to go in an old building even though there is a "No Trespassing" sign. You . . .

☐ Tell them it's wrong and that you'd rather go home.
☐ Go along with the crowd and go in.

You find a wallet with a driver's license and a $50 bill inside. You . . .

☐ Keep it! Must be your lucky day.
☐ Turn it in to the nearest police station so they can get in touch with the owner.

Answers for best choice are on page 167.

Let us not become tired of doing good. At the right time we will gather a crop if we don't give up.

GALATIANS 6:9

Bible Story

ABIGAIL PLEADS FOR NABAL'S LIFE

1 Samuel 25:1-39

A wealthy, but crude and mean, man named Nabal had a sensible and beautiful wife named Abigail.

David and his men had provided help and protection for Nabal's men and their sheep. When they were in need of supplies, David sent ten of his men to Nabal to give him a happy greeting and ask if he could send some supplies to help them. David's men waited for a reply.

Nabal sneered. "Who does David think he is? Why should I give my water and meat to strangers?"

David's men returned to David and told him what Nabal had said.

"Get your swords!" David said. Four hundred men started off with David while 200 remained behind to guard their equipment.

Meanwhile, one of Nabal's servants went to Abigail and told her, "Day and night David and his men were

like a wall of protection to us and the sheep. But Nabal was unkind to David's men. There is going to be trouble for our master and his whole family!"

Abigail quickly gathered supplies and packed them on donkeys. But she didn't tell her husband, Nabal, what she was doing.

When she saw David and his men coming toward her, she quickly got off her donkey and bowed low before him. She said, "I accept all blame in this matter, my Lord. I never saw the young men you sent. Please don't pay any attention to Nabal. He is a foolish man."

Abigail continued. "Please forgive me if I have offended you in any way. I know that God will bless you with success. When he does, please remember me."

David replied, "Praise God! May God bless you for what you have done. You have shown good sense. If you had not hurried out to meet me, not one of Nabal's men would still be alive tomorrow morning." Then David accepted her present and told her, "Return home in peace."

When Abigail arrived home, Nabal was throwing a big party, celebrating like a king. She didn't say anything about David until dawn the next day. When he heard the news, Nabal's heart grew weak. Ten days later, he was dead.

When David heard that Nabal was dead, he sent messengers to Abigail to ask her to become his wife.

Your Turn

1. What did Abigail do after she discovered what Nabal had said to David's men?

2. Name a time you did the right thing and stopped someone from making a terrible mistake.

Do It!

Just as Abigail stopped David from hurting Nabal, you too can do the right thing. Create this framed chalkboard to remind you to never give up doing what is good.

Framed Chalkboard

What You Need

- Picture frame with glass (available at a thrift store or dollar store)
- Newspapers
- Glass cleaner
- Paper towels
- Spray chalkboard paint
- Spray paint of your favorite color
- Chalk

WHAT YOU DO

1. With adult supervision, remove the glass from the picture frame.

2. Lay the glass flat on a paintable surface, such as old newspapers. Do the same with the picture frame, preferably outdoors on a non-windy day.

3. Clean the glass with glass cleaner and paper towels.

4. Spray at least two coats of the chalkboard paint evenly across the glass, allowing the paint to dry between coats.

5. Apply spray paint to your frame with the color of your choice, allowing it to dry between coats.

6. Prime your chalkboard by rubbing the entire thing with the chalk, and then wipe it off.

7. After twenty-four hours, put the glass back in the frame.

8. Write, "Do the Right Thing" on your chalkboard.

9. Hang in your bedroom.

Bible Story

ABIGAIL PLEADS FOR NABAL'S LIFE

1 Samuel 25:1-39

Find the Missing Word

David told Abigail to ___ ___ ___ ___ ___ ___ home in peace. (v. 35)

Write about It

In order to do the right thing, let God transform you by changing the way you think. Use the space below to write (or doodle) about a time you took action and helped someone in need.

Tiny Treasure

When you show respect and follow God's Word, you will be able to make good decisions every day!

Prayer

Lord God, thank you for giving me the courage to not give up. Help me to do the right thing. In Jesus' name, amen.

WHaT IS Pure

> God, create
> a pure heart in me.
> Give me a new spirit
> that is faithful to you.
>
> PSaLM 51:10

Emily's Heart

Every time Emily caught a glimpse of Jasmine, her stomach knotted. Jasmine always seemed to get her way! Now Jasmine had been invited to join the Treble Clef Society and Emily hadn't.

On the bus ride home, Emily slouched in the seat next to her best friend. "This has been the worst day ever!"

"I hate to say this, but you're making a bad situation worse," Ava said. "The only way you're going to get over this whole Jasmine thing is if you let it go." Ava smiled gently.

At her stop, Emily got off and trudged home. She sat on the front steps, her mind reeling from Ava's words. Was she making a bad situation worse? If she was a good sport, she would congratulate Jasmine instead of wishing she'd break her wrist so that Emily could take her place.

God, please forgive me and make my heart clean.
The simple prayer calmed her.

Truth was Emily loved to play the piano, and according to Mrs. Emerson, she had a God-given talent. She'd never give it up, and Miss Forte's decision didn't change that.

The front door opened. "There you are," Mom said.

Emily glanced her mom's direction. "Just needed to think is all."

"Mrs. Emerson called. She wants you to call her back as soon as possible." Emma ran to the phone.

"Oh, I'm so glad you called." Mrs.Emerson said. "I talked with Miss Forte, and she asked if you'd be interested in joining the Treble Clef Society as an intern. She doesn't think your skills are quite ready to be a full-fledged member, but she's willing to spend time with you if you're interested. Before you give me your answer, you must know that I won't be able to be your piano teacher if you decide to take Miss Forte's offer."

Emily hesitated. Mrs. Emerson cut into her thoughts. "Don't let fear stop you from your dreams."

That evening, Emily wrote in her journal.

> Dear God,
>
> Today I was so jealous, and a little bit angry, that I wasn't chosen to be part of the Treble Clef Society. But guess what? Miss Forte wants me after all! I have a lot of work to do, but I'm up for it. I love playing the piano! Yes, I'll miss Mrs. Emerson like crazy, but she said I can come to her house to visit anytime I want.
>
> Love,
>
> Emily

Your Turn

1. Describe a time you were jealous of someone else's accomplishments. How did it make you feel?

2. Write about a situation when you felt disappointed. How did you let it go?

3. Why is it important to keep working toward something even when it seems impossible?

Did You Know?

Anger, bitterness, greed, jealousy, pride, and selfishness are some of the sins that can make your heart unclean. You may look fine on the outside, but God sees the heart. The good news is that he can forgive you and make you clean! But how?

To have a pure heart, give your life to Jesus and ask him to wipe away your sins. But don't stop there. The Bible says, "I keep every thought under control in order to make it obey Christ" (2 Corinthians 10:5). That means being pure in all you think, say, and do by keeping your mind on Jesus.

Ask him to help you make good decisions every day—in what you read, watch, and the games that you play. The right friends can also help you stay pure. Second Timothy 2:22 says, "Try hard to do what is right. Have faith, love and peace. Do these things together with those who call on the Lord from a pure heart." When you choose friends who love God, you will want a pure heart too. By having a pure heart, you will see the good things God gives you (Matthew 5:8).

Try This!

Ask God to forgive you of your sins in order to have a clean heart. Truth is, you can't change on your own. Only God can do that. He will forgive you and change your heart, too.

Below are three ways you can show your devotion to God with a pure heart. But the vowels are missing from some of the words! Replace the vowels so you can remember ways to show your pure heart.

1. Tell God how much you love him. S__ng w__rsh__p s__ngs. __b__y his c__mm__ndm__nts. Pr__y and r__ __d the B__bl__.

2. Be c__nf__d__nt in the person God made you to be. __cc__pt yourself, even the parts you don't like.

3. Show c__mp__ss__ __n to __th__rs with w__rds and __ct__ __ns.

Answer key on page 167.

Do It!

Did you know God loves you and wants you to have a pure heart? Try making this heart puzzle to remind you to be faithful to God.

Heart Puzzle

WHAT YOU NEED

- White cardstock paper
- Black marker
- Pencil
- Crayons or markers
- Scissors
- Envelope

WHAT YOU DO

1. On a piece of white cardstock, draw a large heart with a black marker.

2. With your pencil, draw a picture or design inside the heart. Color it in with your crayons or markers.

3. Cut out the heart with your scissors.

4. Next, cut the heart into puzzle pieces. Be careful not to cut the pieces too small, or else it will make the puzzle too difficult to put together.

5. Put your puzzle together!

6. Store your puzzle in an envelope.

ALTERNATE IDEA

To make it more challenging, do this activity with a friend and exchange puzzles. Or make a bigger puzzle by using a large piece of cardboard.

Blessed are those whose
hearts are pure. They will see God.

MATTHEW 5:8

Bible Story

RUTH WORKS IN BOAZ'S FIELD

Ruth 2

One day, Ruth went out to gather grain left behind by harvesters in a field. She found herself working in a field that belonged to Boaz, a wealthy man. Boaz was a relative of Ruth's father-in-law who had died. Ruth's husband had also died. She was living with her mother-in-law Naomi and trying to gather enough grain so they could eat.

While Ruth was working, Boaz arrived from Bethlehem and greeted the harvesters. Then Boaz asked his foreman, "Who is that young woman over there? Who does she belong to?"

"She is the young woman from Moab who came back with Naomi," the foreman said. "She asked me if she could gather grain behind the harvesters, and has been hard at work ever since."

Boaz went over to Ruth and said, "Stay right behind the young women working in my field. See which part of the field they are harvesting, and then follow them. I have warned the young men not to treat you roughly. And when you are thirsty, help yourself to the water they have drawn from the well."

Ruth fell at his feet and thanked him warmly. "What have I done to deserve such kindness?" she asked. "I am only a foreigner."

"Yes, I know," Boaz replied. "But I also know about everything you have done for Naomi. May the Lord reward you for what you have done."

"You have comforted me by speaking so kindly to me, even though I am not one of your workers," Ruth said.

When Ruth went back to work again, Boaz ordered his young men to let her gather grain right among the sheaves without stopping her. He also instructed them to pull out some heads of barley from the bundles and drop them on purpose for her.

So Ruth gathered barley there all day, and after beating out the grain that evening, collected an entire basket. She carried it back into town and showed it to her mother-in-law.

Naomi asked, "Where did you gather all this grain today?"

Ruth told her about Boaz and the field where she worked.

"May the Lord bless him!" Naomi said. "Boaz is showing kindness to us."

"Boaz also told me to come back and stay with his harvesters until the harvest is completed," Ruth said.

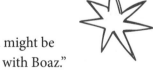

"Good!" Naomi exclaimed. "Do as he said, daughter. You might be bothered by the workers in other fields, but you'll be safe with Boaz."

Your Turn

1. Why did Boaz show kindness to Ruth?

2. How can you have a pure heart and show kindness to others?

Do It!

Just as Ruth showed devotion to her mother-in-law, Naomi, by picking up stalks of grain, you too can show devotion to God by having a pure heart. Create this heart-shaped soap to remind you to ask for forgiveness and be devoted to God.

Heart-Shaped Soap

What You Need

- Large bar of soap
- Dish sponge
- Pencil or marker
- Plastic knife, plastic spoon, and/or craft stick
- Paper plate
- Cup of water
- Paper towels
- Toothpick

WHAT YOU DO

1. Unwrap your bar of soap from the packaging. Run the soap under water and scrub away the brand name with a dish sponge. Let the soap dry overnight.

2. Draw a large heart on the soap with your pencil or marker.

3. With the plastic knife, plastic spoon, and/or craft stick, slowly carve away the excess soap so only your heart remains. Carve over the paper plate to contain the soap shavings.

4. Dip the soap in water, and then dry it off with paper towels. Smooth the sides and edges with your fingers, dipping them in water as needed.

5. Use your toothpick to carve in designs or details.

6. Enjoy!

Bible Story

ГUTH WORKS IN BOAZ'S FIELD

Ruth 2

Find the Missing Word

Boaz spoke ___ ___ ___ ___ ___ ___ to Ruth. (v. 13)

8

Write about It

Being devoted to God means you want to be pure in all you think, say, and do. Use the space below to write (or doodle) about a time you asked Jesus to forgive you and make your heart clean. If you haven't asked before, do it now!

Tiny Treasure

You will have a pure heart when you keep your mind on Jesus.

Prayer

Lord God, thank you for forgiving me when my heart is unclean. Help me to be pure in my thoughts and actions. In Jesus' name, amen.

WHAT IS LOVELY

> Fancy hairstyles don't make you beautiful. Wearing gold jewelry or fine clothes doesn't make you beautiful. Instead, your beauty comes from inside you. It is the beauty of a gentle and quiet spirit. Beauty like this doesn't fade away. God places great value on it.
>
> 1 Peter 3:3–4

Jessica's Unfading Beauty

"Twenty-five. Twenty-six. Twenty-seven." Jessica counted the freckles on her face while looking in the bathroom mirror.

"What are you doing?" Cody, her new seven-year-old foster brother, looked up at her.

"Counting freckles." *Would they ever disappear?* Her best friend, Kayla, didn't have any freckles—or pimples. Not one. Her face was *perfect*!

If Jessica had her way, she wouldn't go to youth group tonight. Besides wearing makeup, several of her friends had gone shopping together and planned to wear their *perfect* outfits, along with their *perfect* jewelry to complete their *perfect* look.

Jessica wasn't allowed to wear makeup yet, hadn't gone shopping for months, and badly needed a haircut. She blew her bangs out of her eyes. How would she fit in? When they got out of the car at church, Mom said, "Jessi, please take Tyler to the preschool room. I'll bring Cody."

Jessica didn't argue. She could take the long way and put off seeing her *perfect* friends.

By the time they reached Tyler's classroom, kids were running around the room, making noise . . . and a big mess. Mrs. Carmichael sat in the corner of the room, fanning her face with a book. She lumbered to her feet and sent Jessica a relieved smile. "Thank goodness help has arrived."

Jessica was already late. The last thing she wanted was to draw attention to herself. Jessica smiled. "What would you like me to do?"

Mrs. Carmichael let out a breath. "Get the snack ready while I read the Bible lesson to the kids."

When the story was over, the kids began to squirm. Jessica set a cup of milk and crackers by each spot at the table—just in time! "Snack time!"

The kids jockeyed for position at the table.

At the end of the class, Mrs. Carmichael raved about what a wonderful helper she was. "Jessica has such a lovely spirit, so gentle and kind. I hope she comes again."

Her words brought a smile to Jessica's face.

Once she got home, she wrote in her journal:

Dear God,

On my way to the car, friends asked me why I didn't go to youth group tonight. I told them that I was needed in my little brother's class and how much fun I had with Mrs. Carmichael. She reminded me that a girl can be lovely on the inside, which is more important than what I wear or how many freckles I have.

Love,

Jessica

Your Turn

1. Is there anything you'd like to change about the way you look? Why?

2. Describe a time you wished you had someone else's hair, clothes, or jewelry. Did your wishes make you feel better?

3. Describe the difference between someone who is only beautiful on the outside and someone who has a gentle and quiet spirit on the inside.

Did You Know?

It's easy to look in the mirror and compare yourself with the images you see in magazines, television, or the movies, but outward beauty doesn't last and is not important to God.

Matthew 6:27–29 says,

> *Can you add even one hour to your life by worrying? And why do you worry about clothes? See how the wild flowers grow. They don't work or make clothing. But here is what I tell you. Not even Solomon in all his royal robes was dressed like one of these flowers.*

Your heavenly Father cares more about what is on the *inside,* or your character, than what is on the outside. It's okay to want to look your best. In fact, brushing your teeth and hair, and wearing clean clothes shows others you're thankful for the body God gave you. But true beauty comes from having a gentle and quiet spirit, which never fades. When you focus on God, you will be more confident in who he made you to be and in his love for you.

Try This!

Having a quiet and gentle spirit takes effort. Ignoring your parents when they are talking or saying rude things is not how God wants you to act. But if you listen to your parents and say kind words, you are being gentle. Jesus was gentle in his words and actions. To have a quiet and gentle spirit like Jesus, ask God to help you.

Below are six steps to be gentle with yourself and others. On each blank line, print a word from the Word Bank to complete each sentence. Each word will be used once.

1. Be _____ with your feelings.

2. _____ before you say or do anything.

3. Learn to _____ about the situation and the people involved.

4. _____ someone else's feelings on the subject.

5. _____ what you are going to do.

6. _____ on all that you've learned.

WORD BANK

care

consider

decide

honest

reflect

think

Do It!

Gentle Sudoku

Instead of counting freckles, try this Sudoku puzzle, and think about how God wants you to focus on inner beauty and having a quiet and gentle spirit. The object of the game is to fill in each box, row, and column with the numbers from one to nine. All nine numbers must be used, and none can be repeated. Use a pencil with a good eraser in case you need to change your answers.

2		9				6		
	4		8	7			1	2
8				1	9		4	
	3		7			8		1
	6	5			8		3	
1				3				7
			6	5		7		9
6		4					2	
	8		3		1	4	5	

Answer key on page 167.

Don't be proud at all. Be
completely gentle. Be patient. Put
up with one another in love.

EPHESIANS 4:2

Bible Story

MaRY BELIEVES GABRIEL'S MESSAGE

Luke 1:26-56

God sent an angel named Gabriel to Mary, a young
virgin engaged to marry a man named Joseph, a
descendent of King David. Gabriel said, "Greetings,
favored woman! The Lord is with you!"

These words confused and disturbed Mary. She tried
to think what the angel could mean. "Don't be afraid,
Mary," the angel said, "for you have found favor with
God! You will conceive and give birth to a son, and
you will name him Jesus. He will be very great and will
be called the Son of the Most High. The Lord God will
give him the throne of this ancestor David. And he will
reign over Israel forever; his kingdom will never end!"

Mary asked the angel, "But how can
this happen? I am a virgin."

The angel replied, "The Holy Spirit will come upon you,
and the power of the Most High will overshadow you.
The baby born to you will be holy, and he will be called

the Son of God. Your relative, Elizabeth, has become pregnant in her old age! People have said she is unable to have a child, but she has conceived a son and is now in her sixth month. For the word of God will never fail."

Mary replied, "I am the Lord's servant. May everything you have said about me come true."

Then Gabriel left her.

A few days later Mary went to Judea, to the town where Elizabeth lived with her husband Zechariah. She entered the house and greeted Elizabeth. At the sound of Mary's voice, Elizabeth's baby leaped within her, and Elizabeth was filled with the Holy Spirit.

Elizabeth hugged Mary and exclaimed, "God has blessed you above all women, and your child is blessed. Why am I so honored that the mother of my Lord should visit me? When I heard your greeting, the baby in my womb jumped for joy. You are blessed because you believed that the Lord would do what he said."

Mary responded with a song of praise we now call "The Magnificat." She stayed with Elizabeth about three months, and then went back to her own home.

Your Turn

1. How did Mary respond when Gabriel told her she was going to have baby Jesus?

2. Look up and read Mary's song in Luke 1:46-56. Write your own song of praise in the space below.

Do It!

Just as Mary believed and trusted God, you too can have an unfading beauty of a gentle and quiet spirit. Create this flower crown and consider how you can love others like Jesus.

Tissue-Paper Flower Crown

WHAT YOU NEED

- Tissue paper in assorted colors, including green
- Ruler
- Scissors
- Green pipe cleaners cut in half
- 1-inch ribbon, enough to go all the way around your head, plus extra to tie in a bow
- Craft glue

WHAT YOU DO

1. To make the flowers, cut the tissue paper into 3x3-inch squares. Each flower uses three pieces of the same color of tissue paper, plus one square of green to look like leaves.

2. Stack the pieces of tissue paper on top of one another, with the green piece on the bottom.

3. Fold the tissue paper like an accordion, back and forth, making three folds (image a).

A

4. Keeping the tissue paper folded, round off the ends with your scissors. Next, wrap a piece of pipe cleaner around the center of the folded tissue paper and twist to secure it (image b).

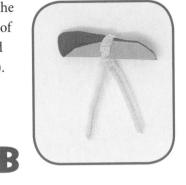

5. To form the petals, open the folds and gently pull up each tissue paper layer towards the center. Do this on both sides.

6. Create as many flowers as you like for your crown.

B

7. Design a pattern for your flowers, such as every other color (pink, lavender, pink, lavender, etc.) or however you choose.

8. Attach the flowers to the ribbon by wrapping the pipe cleaners loosely around the ribbon and twisting to secure them. Tuck the ends of the stems under the flowers.

9. Once you have attached all the flowers, place a small dot of craft glue between the stems of each flower and the ribbon. Let dry.

10. Once dry, tie your flower crown around your head.

Bible Story

MARY BELIEVES GABRIEL'S MESSAGE

Luke 1:26-45

Find the Missing Word

Mary believed what the Lord would do and what he ___ ___ ___ ___.

Write about It

True beauty is when you show love to others. Use the space below to write (or doodle) about a time you chose to be gentle in your words and actions.

Tiny Treasure

When you love others like Jesus, you are lovely like the beautiful scent of a real flower.

Prayer

Lord God, thank you for creating me just as I am. Help me to have a quiet and gentle spirit. In Jesus' name, amen.

WHAT IS ADMIRABLE

> Suppose you can be trusted with something very little. Then you can also be trusted with something very large. But suppose you are not honest with something very little. Then you will also not be honest with something very large.
>
> LUKE 16:10

Lauren's Promise

Lauren sat at the kitchen counter, eating her breakfast.

"Kristi called. She's going on a trip this summer and needs someone to care for her dog," Mom said. Mom's friend Kristi got Max from the animal shelter a few months ago. He was an active little dog with wiry hair and a goofy personality. "Are you up for the job?"

Lauren's eyes widened. "Yes!"

That afternoon, Kristi brought Max, along with his dog stuff, to the house for a trial run. While Max sniffed around the house, Lauren read the letter Kristi wrote about the dog's care. He needed to be fed twice a day, and walked at least once. Kristi warned that he was an active dog and would want to play fetch, and of course needed to be let outside whenever he went by the door. *This is starting to sound like a lot of work!*

The dog jumped up and down from Lauren's bed, chased a ball around the room, and licked everything in sight. Just when Lauren thought Max would never settle down, he twirled around a few times and finally fell asleep on his bed—until the doorbell rang!

Max jumped up and barked at the door.

It was her friend, Emma. "You got a dog?"

"Only for tonight. I'm testing it out to see if I can take care of Max when his owner goes on vacation."

"But my dance recital is tonight. I told you about it weeks ago. You can still come, right?"

Oh no! Lauren wrung her hands. "The only way I'll get my own dog is if I take good care of Max."

"But my dance recital is important. And you promised!"

How could she choose between a dog and her best friend? Lauren bit her lip. "I'm sorry!"

Emma hung her head and walked out the door.

Suddenly Lauren didn't feel right. "Emma, wait!" Lauren called after her.

That night Lauren wrote in her journal.

> **Dear God,**
>
> I told Mom about Emma's dance recital. She said I had a choice to make—go with Emma or take care of Max. I told her I wanted to keep my promise to Emma. Mom said she was proud of me and called Kristi to pick up her dog. I figure I'll start small—like walking the neighbor's dog or getting a different pet. Like a goldfish. Goldfish don't bark!
>
> **Love,**
>
> **Lauren**

Your Turn

1. Do you or someone you know own a pet? Describe it here.

2. Why is it sometimes hard to keep a promise?

3. What small job can you do that can make a big impact on someone's life?

Did You Know?

Faithfulness means doing what you promise. When you are obedient to God and are faithful in the small things, he can trust you with bigger responsibilities.

In Matthew 25:14–29, Jesus tells a parable (story that teaches a lesson) about a man who gives his servants bags of gold.

> To the first servant he gave five bags, to another servant two bags, and to the third servant he gave one bag, each according to their ability. The servant who received five bags put the money to work at once and earned five more. The servant with two bags did the same, and earned two more. But the servant who had one bag, dug a hole and buried his master's money in the ground.

> After a time, the master returned to settle accounts with his servants. To the first servant who he had given five bags and earned five more, the master replied, "Well done, good and faithful servant! You have been faithful with a few things; I will put you in charge of many things. Come and share your master's happiness!"

> To the servant who had two bags and earned two more, the master said, "Well done, good and faithful servant! You have been faithful with a few things; I will put you in charge of many things. Come and share your master's happiness!"

> Then the man who had received one bag of gold said, "Master, I knew you are a hard man, harvesting where you have not sown and gathering where you have not scattered seed. I was afraid and hid your gold. See, here is what belongs to you."

> The master was not happy with the third servant and said, "You wicked, lazy servant! Why didn't you put my money on deposit with the bankers, so that when I returned I would have received it back with interest?" Then he took the bag of gold and gave it to the servant who had ten bags and said,

"For whoever has will be given more, and they will have an abundance. Whoever does not have, even what they have will be taken from them."

God has given each person gifts and talents and wants us to use them for his glory!

Try This!

If you want to be used by God, start by doing the little things first. Below are five ways to build your character so that you can be faithful in the little things. Choose one and in the space provided, doodle what it might look like to do that thing today.

1. Spend time with God every day.
2. Give generously with a grateful heart.
3. Be kind to others.
4. Use your talents to the best of your ability.
5. Finish what you start, whether it is your homework, chores, or something as small as brushing your teeth.

Do It!

Bags of Gold

Try this crossword puzzle to help you remember to be faithful in the small things. Use a pencil to fill in the squares of the crossword puzzle. Have your Bible handy in case you need to look up the parable from Matthew 25:14–29.

across

3. Who did the master give the third slave's bag of gold to? The one who had _____ bags (verse 28).

5. How many bags did the master give the first slave (verse 15)?

7. Who did the master give bags of gold to (verse 14)?

9. What did the master say to the third slave? "You evil, _____ slave" (verse 26).

10. How many bags did the second servant earn (verse 22)?

11. "Everyone who has will be given more. They will have more than _____" (verse 29).

DOWN

1. Who told "The Story of Three Slaves"?

2. How many bags did the master give the third slave (verse 15)?

4. How many bags did the first servant earn (verse 20)?

6. What is a word for a story that teaches a lesson (p. 120 in this book)?

8. What did the master say to the first and second slaves? "Well done, good and _____ slave" (verses 21,23)?

12. How many bags did the third servant earn (verse 24–25)?

Answer key on page 168.

Be sure to have respect for the LORD.
Serve him faithfully. Do it with all your heart.
Think about the great things he has done for you.

1 Samuel 12:24

Bible Story

ESTHER BECOMES QUEEN
Esther 1–2

There was a king named Xerxes who had a beautiful wife named Queen Vashti. One night, she refused to come to the king's party. This greatly angered the king. His advisors suggested a new degree to banish Queen Vashti from the king's presence and to give her position as queen to another woman. The king agreed, deciding to choose a new queen more worthy.

In order to find the new queen Xerxes's attendants suggested, "Let us search the empire to find beautiful young women suitable for you. They should be brought to the royal harem at Susa to be given beauty treatments. Whoever pleases you best will be the new queen." This idea pleased the king.

Meanwhile, in Susa, there was a Jewish man named Mordecai. Mordecai had a beautiful and lovely young cousin named Esther. When her parents had died, Mordecai adopted her into his family and raised her as his very own child.

As a result of the king's new decree, Esther, along with many other beautiful young women were taken to the king's palace. Beauty treatments and special food were given to the women. Immediately, Esther impressed the man in charge. He assigned seven maids to care for Esther.

Because there were people in the land who didn't like Jews, Mordecai instructed Esther to keep her nationality and background a secret. Every day he walked near the courtyard to find out how Esther was and what was happening to her.

After twelve months of beauty treatments, it was Esther's turn to visit the king. Now, the king was attracted to Esther more than anyone and she won his approval. Xerxes was so impressed, he set a royal crown upon her head and made her queen. The king gave a great banquet for all his nobles and officials to celebrate Queen Esther and proclaimed a holiday, distributing gifts throughout the land.

Mordecai became a palace official. Esther continued to keep her nationality and family background a secret according to Mordecai's instruction; listening to him as she had done growing up in his home.

Your Turn

1. Why did Esther keep her nationality and family background a secret?

2. How can you be faithful in little things?

Do It!

Just as Esther was faithful in the little things before she became queen, you too can choose to do what is admirable. Try making this penny necklace and consider how you are God's faithful servant—with your money as well as with your talents.

Penny Necklace

WHaT YOU NeeD

- Hammer
- Nail or awl
- Penny
- Aluminum foil
- Spoon
- Embossing powder
- Small floral decorations (decals, stickers, die cuts, pictures cut from a magazine, etc.)
- Toothpick
- Jump ring and necklace chain

WHaT YOU DO

1. With a parent's help, use a hammer and nail or awl to make a hole through the top of the penny. (Optional: your parent can drill a hole if necessary. They should tape the penny to a block of wood before drilling.)

2. Place the penny on a piece of aluminum foil. Using a spoon, pour some embossing powder on one side of the penny. Follow package instructions to melt the embossing powder. Before it cools completely, stick a toothpick through the hole to make sure it stays open. Allow time to cool.

3. Place floral decorations on the penny.

4. Put embossing powder on top of the decal and melt.

Before it cools completely, stick a toothpick through the hole to make sure it stays open. Allow time to cool.

5. Once cool, place the jump ring through the hole and attach to the necklace chain.

6. Enjoy!

Bible Story

ESTHER BECOMES QUEEN

Esther 1:10–2:18

Find the Missing Word

Esther won the king's ___ ___ ___ ___ ___ ___ ___ ___.

Write about It

Being admirable means being faithful in the little things. Use the space below to write (or doodle) about a time you completed a task well or kept a promise.

Tiny Treasure

When you are faithful with a few things, God will put you in charge of many things!

Prayer

Lord God, thank you for giving me gifts and talents. Help me to be faithful in the little things. In Jesus' name, amen.

Hint: This word means you really like something and it begins with an *a*.

WHaT IS excellent

I pray that your love will grow more and more. And let it be based on knowledge and understanding. Then you will be able to know what is best. Then you will be pure and without blame for the day that Christ returns.

PHILIPPIANS 1:9–10

Savannah's Plan

"Hey, Squirt!" Dad said. "Ready for the movie?"

"Yes!" She loved all the fun places Dad was taking her to since he moved out. They'd been to her favorite Mexican restaurant, out for ice cream, or to the movies, which was today's plan.

On the drive, she saw a group of homeless people holding signs asking for money, pushing grocery carts filled with their stuff, and huddled together under a canopy of trees.

Once inside the theatre, Dad paid for their tickets, a big bucket of popcorn, and two sodas. But Savannah's mind kept drifting to the homeless people she saw on the drive. Did they miss going to the movies? When was the last time they ate buttered popcorn or drank bubbly soda or sat in a comfortable chair?

She brought it up to her dad later that night.

"I love it that you're thinking about others," Dad said.

"I don't just want to *think* about them, Dad. I want to *do* something about it."

129

When Savannah went to bed, she fell asleep to the sound of crickets outside her window, grateful for her full stomach and warm blankets, even if the rest of her room was pretty bare.

The next morning she woke up with a plan. She'd need:

- Toothbrushes
- Toothpaste
- Deodorant
- Lip balm
- Sunscreen

- Trail mix
- Beef jerky
- Socks
- Adhesive bandages
- Travel mugs

Ten minutes later, Savannah ran into the kitchen and told her dad of her plan. "So, what do you think?"

"You're going to need a lot of money for that." Dad sipped his coffee.

"About that . . ." Savannah bit her lip. "Could we go to the dollar store and buy the things on the list instead of going out to eat or to the movies?"

Dad ruffled Savannah's hair. "It's an excellent idea!"

Later, Savannah wrote in her journal:

Dear God,

Wow! What a day! Dad and I made TEN care packages and passed them out to all the homeless people we saw. We learned that they are normal people, like us, and that it was mostly one sad event, like losing a job, that landed them on the street. On top of that, Dad said the next time I visit, instead of spending a bunch of money we'll cook at home and rent a movie. Sounds good to me! Of course, I'd rather he just come back home. Please, God?

Love,

Savannah

Your Turn

1. What needs do you see when you look around?

2. How can you show love to others?

3. What do you like to do? How can you use your gifts and talents to help others?

Did You Know?

God loves you and commands you to show love to others. John 13:34 says, "I give you a new command. Love one another. You must love one another, just as I have loved you." Sometimes it is hard to love someone when you don't even like them, but just as God loves you, you are to love others like Jesus did. He loved his disciples, he loved children, he loved poor people and those with diseases. He loved all kinds of people, even those who were different from him—and difficult to be with.

Try This!

You can love like Jesus by being patient and kind, forgiving others even when they don't deserve it or ask for it, and treating others with honor and respect. By having a heart like Christ, you can show love to family and friends, and even to those who are difficult or different.

Below are fifteen simple ways you can show love to others. Read the list, and then find the underlined words in the word search on the next page.

1. <u>Listen</u> to what people are saying.
2. <u>Offer help</u> when needed.
3. <u>Comfort</u> those who are hurting.
4. <u>Give generously</u> to those in need.
5. <u>Smile</u>!
6. Help your <u>parents</u> with <u>chores</u> around the house.
7. <u>Play</u> the game your <u>sibling</u> wants to play.
8. Bake <u>cookies</u> for your <u>teacher</u>.
9. Draw a <u>picture</u> and send it to a <u>grandparent</u>.
10. Write an <u>encouraging note</u> to a <u>friend</u>.
11. <u>Read</u> a book to someone.
12. Clean up <u>trash</u> in your <u>neighborhood</u>.
13. <u>Invite</u> friends to <u>church</u>.
14. <u>Babysit</u> for <u>FREE</u>!
15. <u>Clean</u> your neighbor's <u>yard</u>.

Circle or draw a line through the
underlined words from page 132.

```
         L K e e            O S F S
       X I V N U B        M S O N I D
     U B S T B P H Y      W J r F T B C C
   M Q N T C O M F O r T G e S M I L e L V
 r S a Q e C H O r e S B F e S G J I D F e W
S P L a Y N K D Y W F a F V J N H H N I H r a J
Y C X C H U r C H J e O D B H B e C G H Q r L N
Y a r D a N P a r e N T S J L r M r L H e L e W
Y D K G r a N D P a r e N T U F Z N O H S L T B
F N F r i e N D B C N e N T S D W T C U S I P D
Z O e L X a a G Z V Z H C r a Y J a a M S V W e
  Y Y I B F r e e L G i e e a W e M P Y X L X
  L a a G I Q L D K P S r N O T e Q B i a N Y
    a G B H Z V C O O K i e S H X a J P X J
      O I Q B T r a S H M a C B B e O T G
      K V U O M e N C O U r a G i N G
        F e P r T N W I i T Y D e N
        M O H H Z i e N U P S P
        V M a O V O V Z N r
          X S Y O S i O D
          N F Y D T r
          X Q S e
          H F
```

Answer key on page 168.

Do It!

Fill in the blanks to write a short story about showing love to others using the ways listed on page 132. Then, draw a picture to illustrate your story in the space on page 135.

One day, _____ called me over and asked if I could help. At first, I
              who

didn't want to _____ because I wanted to _____ instead.
           action   action

I was about to complain, when I remembered John 13:34. It says, "You must

love one another, just as I have loved you." So I decided to love like Jesus and

_____ even though I didn't feel like it. Guess what? By helping
    action

_____, I discovered helping others could be a lot of fun!
    who

The next day, I spotted _____, who needed help to
                        who

_____, and so I jumped in to help. I _____ and
    who   action

_____ until I couldn't _____ anymore.
    action   action

The following day, I saw _____, and _____ needed
                       who   who

help. So I grabbed an _____ and started to _____.
object   action

_____ was so happy that I _____ and told
who   action

me that I should _____ more often because I was so good at
action

_____. It made me feel good to help _____ that
action   action

I decided to _____ every week. By helping _____,
action   who

I discovered what I love to do most! And that is _____!
action

"Love the Lord your God with all your heart and with all your soul. Love him with all your mind and with all your strength." And here is the second one. "Love your neighbor as you love yourself." There is no commandment more important than these."

Mark 12:30–31

Bible Story

AENEAS AND DORCAS

Acts 9:32–42

After Jesus returned to Heaven, his friends traveled the world to tell others about God's love and how Jesus died so that we could be members of God's family.

One of Jesus' friends, Peter, was traveling and helping people. He came to the town of Lydda to visit the Lord's people there. There he met a man named Aeneas. Aeneas was paralyzed and had been unable to get out of bed for eight years.

"Aeneas," Peter said to him, "Jesus Christ heals you. Get up and roll up your mat." Immediately, Aeneas got up. All those who lived in Lydda and Sharon saw him. They were so amazed! They must have known that Peter served the one true God. The people wanted to know about God, so they all decided to follow Jesus.

Meanwhile, in Joppa there was a disciple named Tabitha. Her name was Dorcas in Greek. Dorcas was always doing good and helping poor people. But sadly, she became sick and died. Her body was washed and placed in an upstairs room of her house.

Lydda was near Joppa; so when the people who followed Jesus heard that Peter was in Lydda, they sent two men to Peter and begged him to come at once.

When he got there, a group of widows was crying. They showed Peter all the clothes Dorcas had made to give to others and help them. Everyone was so sad that Dorcas had died.

Peter felt sorry for all the sad people. He sent everyone out of the room. He then got down on his knees and prayed. He turned toward the dead woman, and said, "Tabitha, get up." She opened her eyes, and seeing Peter she sat up. He took her hand and helped her stand to her feet.

Then he called for the people who had sent for him, especially the widows, and presented Dorcas to them—alive! This amazing news became known all over Joppa, and as a result, many people decided to follow Jesus.

Your Turn

1. Who did Peter heal in this story? Describe them.

2. How can you be like Dorcas (Tabitha) and show kindness to others?

Do It!

Just as Dorcas showed compassion to others by doing good and helping the poor, you too can choose what is excellent. Try making this rain chain and consider how your love can overflow to others.

Mini Clay Pot Rain Chain

WHaT YOU NeeD

- Newspapers
- 10 mini clay pots
- Outdoor acrylic paint
- Paintbrush or paint sponge
- 10 large round beads
- Zip ties from the dollar store, both large and small
- Hook

WHaT YOU DO

1. Set newspapers on your table to keep the area clean.

2. Paint the inside and the outside of the mini clay pots with the outdoor acrylic paint. Allow time to dry.

3. Attach a large plastic bead to a small zip tie and fasten (image a). Repeat, making ten, one for each clay pot.

4. Place the painted clay pots in a row

A

vertically on the table, leaving a few inches between each pot. Next, set the fastened zip ties (with large beads attached) directly below each pot (image b).

5. Create the rain chain by making a loop with a large zip tie. Link a small zip tie around the large one and then thread it through the hole of the first mini clay pot, attaching it to the small zip tie with a bead (image c).

B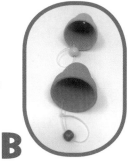

6. Repeat this process through all the remaining pots.

7. Hang the rain chain by hooking the top loop on a hook near the rain gutter on your house, or in a tree.

8. On a stormy day, watch the rain fill the mini pots and trickle down the chain.

C

Bible Story

aeneas and Dorcas

Acts 9:32-42

Find the Missing Word

Dorcas ___ ___ ___ ___ ___ ___ helped those in need.

Write about It

Doing what is excellent means showing love to others, even those who might be different or difficult. Use the space below to write (or doodle) about a time your love overflowed to someone in need.

Tiny Treasure

Jesus showed love to all kinds of people, and wants you to do the same.

Prayer

Lord God, thank you for loving me. Help me to love others like Jesus. In Jesus' name, amen.

WHAT IS WORTHY OF PRAISE

> My people, you will go out
> of Babylon with joy. You will be led
> out of it in peace. The mountains and hills
> will burst into song as you go. And all
> the trees in the fields will clap their hands.
>
> ISaIaH 55:12

Brianna's Discovery

At camp Friday morning, Brianna tiredly followed the cabin leader
to the cafeteria. Loud voices filled the room. Brianna grabbed a
plate of scrambled eggs and bacon and joined her friends.

"There you are!" Hannah scooted over and made room for
Brianna on the bench. "I thought you'd never get here."

"I almost slept in." Brianna sat beside her.

"Well, it's a good thing you didn't," Hannah said. "I hear the waterfall is amazing!"

We'll see about that, Brianna thought. Her mom had told her that she
wasn't a morning person. *Guess Mom was right.* Brianna decided she'd
better change her attitude if she was going to enjoy the two-mile hike.

On the walk, the nature guide talked about the trees, rocks, plants, animals, and how God made them all. More than once, Brianna was amazed at God's creation. She reached down and picked up a leaf, twirling it between her fingers.

They crossed a small creek, jumped on some rocks, and headed up the trail. Only a mile to go before they reached the waterfall! Hannah's excitement was rubbing off on her.

She tugged on Hannah's arm. "Come on! Let's hurry and get toward the front."

Hannah hurried to keep up. "Why the rush?"

Instead of answering, Brianna continued to pull her friend up the hill, laughing all the way.

The sound of water rushing, hitting rocks, and landing with a splash below pushed Brianna around the last bend in the trail. The waterfall was more beautiful than Brianna imagined. Now she understood why people came from all over the state to hike the trail. Before they hiked back down, the leaders taught them a worship song about how God's love is like a waterfall, wild and free.

That night Brianna grabbed her flashlight and wrote in her journal.

> **Dear God,**
>
> The waterfall was AMAZING!!! Can you believe I hiked four miles today? It was tough, but so worth it! Truthfully, I didn't want to be left behind, but I'm not used to going to camp and having so many people around. The best part about the hike was singing worship songs on the trail. Yep, we even sang the whole way back to camp! Your creation makes us sing! Thank you, God, for nature—and for making me.
>
> **Love,**
>
> **Brianna**

Your Turn

1. What do you think you'd enjoy about camp?

2. When was the last time you had a bad attitude? Write about it here.

3. Name one or more things God created that is worthy of praise.

Did You Know?

You don't have to wait until you go to church on Sunday to praise God. Psalm 104:33 says, "I will sing to the LORD all my life. I will sing praise to my God as long as I live." You can praise God in your room, lying in your bed, taking a shower, or just about anywhere. Wow, that's a lot of singing!

But if you don't like to sing, don't worry! You can still worship God by listening to the words and saying them in your head. But here's the thing—you don't have to have a perfect singing voice to praise God. Because the truth is, praising God is about showing God how much you love him.

Try This!

Worshiping God is good for YOU! You'll be amazed at how much joy you'll have and how much your faith will grow when you praise him. By worshiping God, you are declaring that you believe in him and want to please him.

On the next page are five ways to praise God. Choose one and illustrate it on page 145.

1. PRAISE GOD WITH DANCING AND MUSICAL INSTRUMENTS. "Let them praise his name with dancing. Let them make music to him with harps and tambourines" (Psalm 149:3).

2. PRAISE GOD WITH YOUR HANDS. "Lift up your hands in the temple and praise the LORD" (Psalm 134:2).

3. PRAISE GOD WITH YOUR VOICE. "Praise the LORD. How good it is to sing praises to our God! How pleasant and right it is to praise him!" (Psalm 147:1).

4. PRAISE GOD WITH YOUR WORDS. "So let us never stop offering to God our praise through Jesus. Let us talk openly about our faith in him. Then our words will be like an offering to God" (Hebrews 13:15).

5. PRAISE GOD WITH OTHERS. "I will announce your name to my people. I will praise you among those who are gathered to worship you" (Psalm 22:22).

Do It!

Draw pictures of the places you go throughout the day. Under each picture, write down a way you can praise God in that location.

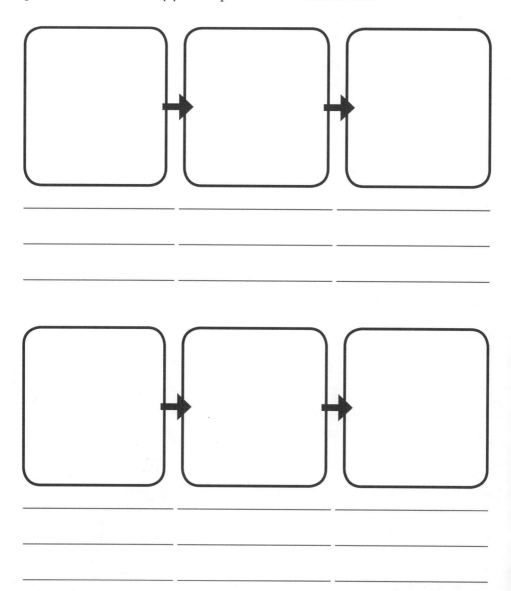

Shout for joy to the LORD, everyone on earth. Worship the LORD with gladness. Come to him with songs of joy. Know that the LORD is God. He made us, and we belong to him. We are his people. We are the sheep belonging to his flock. Give thanks as you enter the gates of his temple. Give praise as you enter its courtyards. Give thanks to him and praise his name. The LORD is good. His faithful love continues forever. It will last for all time to come.

PSALM 100

Bible Story

JESUS ANOINTED BY A SINFUL WOMAN
Luke 7:36-50

Jesus was having dinner at the home of a Pharisee. He was reclined at the table when a woman appeared. She was a woman who lived a sinful life. She had learned that Jesus was having dinner there and came with an alabaster jar of perfume. She stood and wept at his feet, wetting his feet with her tears. Then she wiped them with her hair, kissed them, and poured perfume on them.

When the Pharisee who had invited Jesus saw this, he said to himself, *If this man really was a prophet, he would know who is touching him and what kind of woman she is—a sinner.*

Jesus said, "Simon, I have something to tell you."

"Tell me, teacher," Simon said.

"Two people owed money to a certain moneylender. One owed him five hundred denarii, and the other fifty. Neither of them had the money to pay him back, so he forgave the debts of both. Now which man will love him more?"

Simon replied, "I suppose the one who had the bigger debt forgiven."

"You have judged correctly," Jesus said. Then he indicated the woman. "Do you see this woman? I came into your house. You did not give me any water for my feet, but she wet my feet with her tears and wiped them with her hair. You did not give me a kiss, but this woman has not stopped kissing my feet. You did not put oil on my head, but she has poured perfume on my feet. Therefore, I tell you, her many sins have been forgiven—as her great love has shown. But those who have been forgiven little, love little."

Then Jesus said to her,
"Your sins are forgiven."

The other guests began to say
among themselves, "Who is
this who even forgives sins?"

Jesus said to the woman,
"Your faith has saved
you; go in peace."

Your Turn

1. What did the woman pour on Jesus's feet? Why?

2. How can you show your love to God today?

Do It!

Just as the woman worshiped at Jesus's feet, you too can worship God by your words and actions. Try making this Sheet Music Watercolor Art and consider how you can praise your Father in Heaven.

Sheet Music Art

WHAT YOU NEED

- Computer or cell phone, printer, and colored paper
- Acrylic paint
- Paintbrush
- Canvas
- Pencil
- Scissors
- Decoupage medium (Mod Podge, white glue and water, etc.)
- Cotton swabs

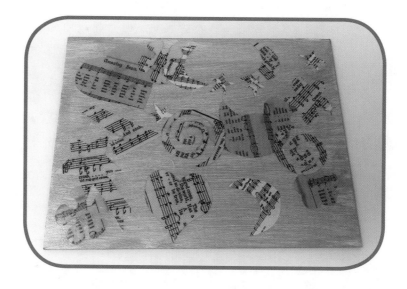

WHAT YOU DO

1. Search online for "public domain hymns sheet music." Choose a hymn, download and print the sheet music on colored paper.

2. Paint canvas a color you haven't used on the sheet music for contrast. Allow time to dry.

3. On the backside of the different colored sheet music, use pencil to draw simple designs, such as a heart, butterfly, bird, musical notes, or anything else you can think of.

4. Cut out the designs.

5. Arrange your designs on the canvas. You may overlap the designs or leave space between them.

6. Decoupage the designs in place with your paintbrush, then lightly brush the decoupage medium all over the canvas, including the top of the designs. Be careful not to get it too gluey or else you might smear the paint. (If you do, use a wet cotton swab to clean it up.) Let dry.

7. Hang your canvas in your room and enjoy!

ALTERNATE IDEA

- Instead of (or in addition to) decoupaging the decorated sheet music to a canvas, consider decoupaging a cardboard or wooden box.
- Use stencils to create your sheet-music shapes.

Bible Story

JESUS ANOINTED BY A SINFUL WOMAN

Luke 7:36-50

Find the Missing Word

The woman poured perfume on Jesus's feet from an

___ ___ ___ ___ ___ ___ ___ ___ ___ jar.

Write about It

Worshiping God means having a sincere devotion to the Lord with a grateful heart. Use the space below to write (or doodle) your own song of praise.

Tiny Treasure

God made everything and is worthy of praise!

Prayer

Lord God, thank you that I get to worship such an amazing God! Help me to praise you always. In Jesus' name, amen.

GOD'S PEACE

May the God who gives hope fill you with great joy. May you have perfect peace as you trust in him. May the power of the Holy Spirit fill you with hope.

ROMANS 15:13

Emily's Hope

The whole way home, Emily stared out the window. She and her parents had just met with her math teacher, Mr. McPherson. "Emily hasn't been handing in her homework and has a hard time focusing," Mr. McPherson had said. "There is a tutor available after school a few times a week."

Her stomach tightened. She didn't have time to go to a math tutor when she needed to practice the piano. Last week Miss Forte had praised her for her dedication. What would she think of Emily now?

That night at dinner, Emily swirled her spaghetti around her plate.

"I called Miss Forte and told her you were having trouble with math," Sandy, her step-mom, said.

Emily's mouth dropped open. "You didn't . . . "

Sandy's voice softened. "She understands that school comes before piano. She said you can continue your internship with the Treble Clef Society after you've completed your math assignments and have caught up with the rest of your class."

"But that could take all year." Emily blinked back tears. "You know how important the Treble Clef Society is to me!"

Dad leaned forward in his chair. "I'm sorry, honey, but like Miss Forte said, school comes first. Tutoring starts tomorrow."

Emily pushed herself away from the kitchen table. "So besides kids at school knowing I need a math tutor, now everyone in the Treble Clef Society will know, too?" She raced to her room and flopped back on her bed. *Stupid math!* "God, don't you care about me?" The short prayer shot out of her mouth.

At the end of the next school day, Mr. McPherson sent her to the library ten minutes before the bell rang. When she walked into the library, she spotted a small group of kids gathering at the far table.

A high school boy with dark curly hair and glasses motioned her over. "You must be Emily," he said.

It took her a minute to answer because she not only recognized all the kids at the table, but her friend Ava was there, too!

"Okay, everybody. Let's get started."

That night Emily wrote in her journal,

Dear God,

Tutoring wasn't so bad. It's funny how no one wants other people to know when they need help. Truth is everyone needs help sometimes. And the only way we can have peace in our hearts is if we trust in you!

Love,

Emily

Your Turn

1. Name a time you needed help with your schoolwork.

2. Why is it hard to ask for help?

3. How can you have joy and peace during difficult times?

Did You Know?

You can have joy and peace when you keep your eyes on Jesus and trust in him.

Isaiah 26:3 says, "Lord, you will give perfect peace to those who commit themselves to be faithful to you. That's because they trust in you."

Talk to God and tell him what's on your mind, and remember Philippians 4:4–8:

> *Always be joyful because you belong to the Lord. I will say it again. Be joyful! Let everyone know how gentle you are. The Lord is coming soon. Don't worry about anything. No matter what happens, tell God about everything. Ask and pray, and give thanks to him. Then God's peace will watch over your hearts and your minds. He will do this because you belong to Christ Jesus. God's peace can never be completely understood.*

> *Finally, my brothers and sisters, always think about what is true. Think about what is noble, right and pure. Think about what is lovely and worthy of respect. If anything is excellent or worthy of praise, think about those kinds of things.*

Try This!

When you seek God first, you will have joy and peace. Matthew 6:33 says, "Put God's kingdom first. Do what he wants you to do. Then all those things will also be given to you."

Below are seven ways that will help you learn to trust in God. Place the underlined words below in the crossword puzzle. **Hint:** Start with the words with the most letters.

1. READ your Bible and ask God for help.
2. CHOOSE to TRUST in God instead of yourself.
3. PRAY and give your day to him.
4. REMEMBER all your BLESSINGS come from God.

5. GIVE to others.

6. ADMIT your mistakes.

7. THINK about how much God LOVES you!

Answer key on page 168.

Do It!

Treasure Clues

Decode the clues in this treasure hunt for items Emily might find in her desk.

1. Pen + child—hd + s = ___ ___ ___ ___ ___ ___ ___

2. Egg—gg + rat—t + ser = ___ ___ ___ ___ ___ ___

3. Ape—e + pole—o = ___ ___ ___ ___ ___

4. Chalk—hk + cup—p + alligator—alig = ___ ___ ___ ___ ___ ___ ___ ___ ___

5. Shoes—Sho + salt—lt + y = ___ ___ ___ ___ ___

Now circle the first letter in each word you found. Place the circled letters in order on the spaces below to remind you what the Lord gives you when you trust in God and are faithful to him.

SEEK GOD FIRST AND YOU WILL HAVE ___ ___ ___ ___ ___

Answer key on page 168.

The LORD gives me strength.
He is like a shield that keeps me
safe. My heart trusts in him, and
he helps me. My heart jumps for
joy. With my song I praise him.

PSALM 28:7

Bible Story

JESUS CALMS THE STORM

Mark 4:35-41

One evening, after a long and tiring day, Jesus said to his disciples, "Let us go over to the other side of the Sea of Galilee." Leaving the crowd behind, they all set sail in the boat. There were several boats, as each boat could only hold a few people. Jesus got in one of the boats, laid down, and fell fast asleep.

There was a sudden gust of wind, followed quickly by another. A furious storm rapidly came up. Waves broke over the boat, and the boat was nearly swamped. Jesus was in the back of the boat, still sleeping on a cushion. The disciples weren't asleep. They were awake and terrified! The men woke Jesus, asking him, "Teacher, don't you care if we drown?"

Jesus woke up. Perhaps his disciples expected him to grab a bucket and start bailing. Or maybe they thought he would tell them which sails to raise or lower, direct them which way to turn the boat . . . something!

When Jesus got up, he did something they never expected. Jesus rebuked the wind and said to the waves, "Quiet! Be still!" Then the wind died down and it was completely calm. Jesus completely stopped the storm—with only his words!

Jesus turned to his disciples and asked them, "Why are you so afraid? Do you still have no faith?"

The disciples were in absolute awe of what they'd just witnessed. They had seen Jesus heal people and do many amazing things. But now they'd seen him control the weather. They looked at each other and asked, "Who is this? Even the wind and the waves obey him!"

Your Turn

1. Why were the disciples afraid even though Jesus was with them?

2. A storm doesn't have to be a weather event. A storm could be anything that upsets your life and creates problems for you. Name a storm that is going on in your life right now. How can you trust God during this time?

Do It!

Just as Jesus calmed the stormy seas and brought peace to the disciples, you too can trust him during difficult times. Try making this confetti bowl and consider how you can be filled with God's peace every day.

Confetti Bowl

WHAT YOU NEED

- Balloon
- Large plastic container
- Decoupage medium
- Plate
- Foam brush
- Confetti
- Scissors

WHAT YOU DO

1. Blow up the balloon and tie off the end.

2. Place the balloon in a plastic container to hold it in place. Be sure to place it with the knot inside the container.

3. Squirt or pour decoupage medium onto a plate.

4. Spread decoupage medium over the top half of the balloon with a foam brush.

5. Sprinkle half a bag of confetti all over the decoupage medium (image a). Allow time to dry.

6. While drying, pour any spilled confetti back into the bag.

7. Once dry, repeat Steps 4–6, completing steps four or more times. Wait for the bowl to dry between coats of decoupage medium.

8. After the final coat is dry (image b), cut the neck of the balloon (under the knot) and remove.

9. Fill your bowl. Enjoy!

A

B

OPTIONAL

- Make your own confetti by using a hole punch and different colors of paper.
- Trim the bowl with scissors for a smooth edge.

Bible Story

JESUS CALMS THE STORM

Mark 4:35-41

Find the Missing Word

Even the wind and the waves ___ ___ ___ ___ Jesus.

Write about It

Asking God to help you is the first step to finding true joy and peace. Use the space below to write (or doodle) about a time you trusted him to help you.

Tiny Treasure

Jesus will give you joy and peace because you trust in him.

Prayer

Lord God, thank you for filling my heart with joy. Help me to trust in you. In Jesus' name, amen.

Answer Keys

Find the Missing Word

Week 1, page 20: Job was an honest man. (B)

Week 2, page 32: The Samaritan showed mercy. (e)

Week 3, page 44: God heard Elijah's prayer. (j)

Week 4, page 56: Hannah prayed to the Lord. (o)

Week 5, page 68: Rebekah told Jacob to bring her two fine young goats. (y)

Week 6, page 80: The Lord forbade David to kill Saul. (f)

Week 7, page 92: David told Abigail to return home in peace. (u)

Week 8, page 104: Boaz spoke kindly to Ruth. (l)

Week 9, page 116: Mary believed what the Lord would do and what he said. (a)

Week 10, page 128: Esther won the king's approval. (l)

Week 11, page 140: Dorcas always helped those in need. (w)

Week 12, page 152: The woman poured perfume on Jesus's feet from an alabaster jar. (a)

Week 13, page 164: Even the winds and the waves obey Jesus. (y)

Secret Message: Be joyful always!

Week I, Try This!

Page 13

1. wheelbarrow
2. garden trowel
3. garden gloves
4. pruning shears
5. loppers
6. garden hose
7. garden fork
8. leaf rake
9. square point shovel
10. spade

Character Dot-to-Dot

Page 14

Scrambled Senses

PAGE 38

1. You can *see* the snow-capped *mountains*.

2. You can hear the *wind* rustling the *leaves* on the *trees*.

3. You can smell the beautiful *flowers*.

4. You can *taste* an apple from an apple tree.

5. You can touch the cool ocean *water* or the *grass* beneath bare feet.

Lord's Prayer Word Search

PAGE 50

```
Y M M F O R G I V E W T O D A Y A Y
K N T F Y B A H E A V E N Z Z B P U
Z T Q S D K A G T B K G I V E N T K
T E F A D A I A A P Q K Y H K S C I
H M O V H G I V H I K E E P K I H N
D P R E A O O L K M N Q X B R N A G
O T G K W A N T Y V V S R B C S P D
N E I Y G H B O B I N N T I D I P O
E D V E A R T H R Y F A T H E R E M
D W E P D K R A K E Y M T Z Q G N E
H Y N W Z K Y R S H D E B R E A D E
S G W R R K O M E V I L U S R G A V
```

Week 5, Try This!

PAGE 61

1. Read the Bible

2. Pray!

3. Ask questions.

4. Be honest.

5. Write down your feelings

6. Speak the truth in love.

7. . . . talk with an adult . . .

Truth Maze

PAGE 62

Truthful words last forever. But lies last for only a moment (Proverbs 12:19).

Decision Quiz

PAGE 74

1. B or C

2. B

3. A

4. B

5. C

Bravery Quiz

PAGE 86

The best choices are:

1. Ask an adult to help you find the lost dog's owner.
2. Talk to your friend and encourage her to be nice.
3. Cover your paper with your hand.
4. Tell them it's wrong and that you'd rather go home.
5. Turn the wallet in to the nearest police station so they can get in touch with the owner.

Week 8, Try This!

PAGE 97

1. Tell God how much you love him. Sing worship songs. Obey his commandments. Pray and read the Bible.
2. Be confident in the person God made you to be. Accept yourself, even the parts you don't like.
3. Show conpassion to others with words and actions.

Week 9, Try This!

PAGE 109

1. Be **honest** with your feelings.
2. **Reflect** before you say or do anything.
3. Learn to **care** about the situation and the people involved.
4. **Consider** someone else's feelings on the subject.
5. **Decide** what you are going to do.
6. **Think** on all that you've learned.

Gentle Sudoku

PAGE 110

2	1	9	5	4	3	6	7	8
5	4	3	8	7	6	9	1	2
8	7	6	2	1	9	3	4	5
4	3	2	7	6	5	8	9	1
7	6	5	1	9	8	2	3	4
1	9	8	4	3	2	5	6	7
3	2	1	6	5	4	7	8	9
6	5	4	9	8	7	1	2	3
9	8	7	3	2	1	4	5	6

Bags of Gold

PAGE 122

ACROSS

3. ten

5. five

7. slaves

9. lazy

10. two

11. enough

DOWN

1. Jesus

2. one

4. five

6. parable

8. faithful

12. none

Week II, Try This!

PAGE 132

Week 13, Try This!

PAGE 157

Treasure Clues

PAGE 158

1. Pen + child—hd + s = **pencils**

2. Egg—gg + rat—t + ser = **eraser**

3. Ape—e + pole—o = **apple**

4. Chalk—hk + cup—p + alligator—alig = **calculator**

5. Shoes—Sho + salt—lt + y = **essay**

Seek God first and you will have **peace**.

168